933
φιλ gen
A6R

PRENTICE-HALL CONTEMPORARY
PERSPECTIVES IN PHILOSOPHY SERIES

Joel Feinberg and Wesley C. Salmon, *editors*

Alan Ross Anderson	MINDS AND MACHINES
V. C. Chappell	ORDINARY LANGUAGE
Nelson Pike	GOD AND EVIL
George Pitcher	TRUTH
Vincent Tomas	CREATIVITY IN THE ARTS

D1438031

TRUTH

Edited by

GEORGE PITCHER
Princeton University

CONTEMPORARY PERSPECTIVES
IN PHILOSOPHY SERIES

PRENTICE-HALL, INC. Englewood Cliffs, New Jersey

Prentice-Hall International, Inc., *London*
Prentice-Hall of Australia, Pty., Ltd., *Sydney*
Prentice-Hall of Canada, Ltd., *Toronto*
Prentice-Hall of India (Private) Ltd., *New Delhi*
Prentice-Hall of Japan, Inc., *Tokyo*

© 1964
by PRENTICE-HALL, INC.
Englewood Cliffs, N.J.

Current printing (last digit):

12 11 10 9 8 7

Library of Congress Catalog Card Number:
64-11556

Printed in the United States of America
C-93219

CONTEMPORARY PERSPECTIVES

IN PHILOSOPHY

This series is designed to provide a wide group of readers with collections of essays by contemporary philosophers on problems presently under active discussion in philosophical circles. The articles have been carefully selected for their lucidity and intelligibility, revealing the vitality of current philosophy to an audience which would not normally have recourse to professional journals. Each volume consists of articles devoted to a single topic, thereby creating an unusual degree of internal coherence and dialectical unity. In many cases the articles are addressed to one another as replies or rebuttals, or are otherwise built upon earlier essays to carry the discussion forward to new levels of clarity. The editor of each volume contributes an introduction which furnishes the reader with the orientation and general framework for a full understanding of the issues. Although each volume is deliberately restricted in scope, the series as a whole ranges over the entire breadth of philosophy, from aesthetics and philosophy of religion to semantics and philosophy of science.

The series is dedicated to the view that contemporary philosophical perspectives—even on ancient problems—are distinctive, exciting, and fully intelligible to students and other nonprofessionals. The volumes are designed for use as supplementary materials or as components in larger "homemade" anthologies, in both introductory and advanced courses, and for use as basic source materials for student research projects. They enable the teacher to expose students to current philosophy without the usual struggle over library copies of journals. In addition, these anthologies will be useful to scholars in fields bordering on philosophy—for example, law, linguistics, literature, mathematics, physics, psychology, and theology—who wish to find in convenient capsule form the best of recent philosophical thinking on subjects of interest to them. For readers in general, the series provides an opportunity to sample the actual substance and methods of contemporary philosophy.

Joel Feinberg
Princeton University

Wesley C. Salmon
Indiana University

CONTENTS

TRUTH

INTRODUCTION

GEORGE PITCHER

Truth is the concern of all honest men: they try to espouse only *true* assertions, claims, theories, and so on. This is truth in extension. Philosophers worry also about truth in intension—i.e., about the concept of truth or the meaning of the term 'truth.' The great philosophers of history, however, although they had something to say about this concept, said surprisingly little: they were far more interested in truths than in 'truth.' It was not until the end of the nineteenth century that the subject was discussed earnestly and with great thoroughness. The stimulus for this sudden late outburst was, I think, the apparently outrageous things which the Absolute Idealists of the middle and late nineteenth century said about truth. Interest in the subject has not seriously flagged since then, and was vigorously freshened by the Austin-Strawson debate of 1950.

The works presented here deal with several important philosophical issues connected with the notion of truth. But many other relevant topics have regrettably had to be ignored. Most notably perhaps, there is no

1

discussion of the coherence, pragmatic, and semantic conceptions of truth. (Substantial bibliographies for all of them are given at the end of the book, however.)

The pieces fall into two groups. The subject of the first, consisting of the first five selections, is the Austin-Strawson debate, which is itself included. The second group comprises the last three selections. Michael Dummett's article is concerned largely with issues raised by Peter Strawson in the two selections which precede it—although Dummett also has interesting things to say about Ramsey's "redundancy theory" and about the connection between meaning and truth.

In the remainder of this introduction, I shall try to describe some—by no means all—of the pitfalls that earlier philosophers have fallen into or at least, given their views, *ought* to have fallen into, in thinking about truth. My hope is that this background will afford both a better understanding of why the writers represented here go about their business in the way they do, and a heightened appreciation of the magnitude of their achievements.

People think and assert many things, some of which are true and others false. (Many are neither true nor false; but that important fact can be ignored for the present.) If a person thinks or asserts something true, what is there about what he thinks or says that makes it true? What, in short, is truth? These questions can seem unspeakably deep; they can also seem unspeakably trivial. That is one good sign that they are philosophical. Another is that they are puzzling. On the surface, they are not puzzling, but the deeper one goes, the more puzzling they become.

The question "What is truth?" presents the aspect of a blank and very high wall: one is reduced to staring at it helplessly. Abstract substantives often produce this effect in philosophy. What we must evidently do is spurn the noble but abstract noun in favor of the more humble adjective: 'truth,' after all, is just 'true' plus '-th.' Let us ask, then: What is it for something a person says or thinks to be true? Some moves now at least seem possible. This freedom affords only brief comfort, however; for the natural moves we are tempted to make turn out either to be just wrong or to run into great obstacles.

For example: since 'true' is an adjective, one might naturally be tempted to suppose that it designates a property. In "What she wore was magenta," 'magenta' designates a property of what she wore; in "What he stepped on was sticky," 'sticky' designates a property of what he stepped on; so why shouldn't 'true' in "What he said (or thought) was true" designate a property of what he said (or thought)? G. E. Moore (1873-1958) succumbed to this temptation: he admitted that he once held the view—on grounds, presumably, like those which led him to the corresponding view about goodness—that truth is a "simple unanalyzable property." [1] Bertrand Russell at one point asserted a similar doctrine,[2] although as the grammatical illusion worked on him, he saw two simple properties, truth and falsehood, where Moore had seen but one: falsehood for Moore was the mere absence of truth, and so, like all evil, nothing positive, but mere negation or deficiency.

But if falsehood is a deficiency, one thing that seems obvious is that the theory of truth as a simple quality is itself sadly deficient. It has no shred of plausibility for the important case of contingent truths (such as "John is in town," "It is raining") ; because it implies that in order to discover that they are true, one has only to examine them to determine that they possess the requisite simple property, and that is absurd. And even in the case of necessary truths (such as "$2 + 2 = 4$"), where the view does at least have a measure of initial plausibility, it still leads to paradoxical results. For example, the question "What makes it true that $2 + 2 = 4$?" must surely make plain sense and have some kind of informative answer; yet according to the view under discussion it is a very strange question indeed and has no such answer. On the simple property view, the only possible kind of reply would be "It just is, that's all. What do you mean?" Similarly, assuming that yellowness is a simple property, the question "What makes this cloth yellow?" is a strange question to which the most appropriate answer is the uninformative one "It just is, that's all. What do you mean?" The question about yellowness, in fact, is actually far less strange than the corresponding one about truth would be, for it might mean "What substance is present in this cloth, or what chemical process is it subjected to, to make it yellow?," whereas on the simple property view of truth, there seems to be no such plausible way to construe the corresponding question about truth.[3] But surely questions of the form "What makes it true that S is P?," where "S is P" is a necessary truth, make perfectly good sense and have informative answers.

The basic dissatisfaction we feel with the simple property view can be put like this: it seems perfectly clear that what makes the thought that $2 + 2 = 4$ true cannot, as the view requires, be something inherent in the thought itself, as if the nature of the numbers 2 and 4 had nothing

---

[1] G. E. Moore, "Beliefs and Propositions," *Some Main Problems of Philosophy* (New York: The Macmillan Company, 1953), p. 261.

[2] Bertrand Russell, "Meinong's Theory of Complexes and Assumptions," Part III, *Mind*, XIII (1904), 423f.

[3] It might possibly be held that truth is a simple property attaching only to what Moore called *organic wholes* [See his *Principia Ethica* (London: Cambridge University Press, 1903), pp. 27ff.], in which case the question could be plausibly construed; but I do not see how the doctrine of organic wholes *could* be applied here in the area of truth.

whatever to do with it; on the contrary, we are strongly inclined to suppose that what makes it true must be something about the numbers 2 and 4 and their relationship to one another. We think that what makes the thought true is the fact that $2 + 2$ *does* equal 4—however the expression 'the fact that . . .' is to be understood.

It appears, then, that we must shut our eyes to the misleading grammatical form of such sentences as "What he said is true" and "Your belief is true," which makes it look as though 'true' were the name of a property which may belong to what people say or think, and try to construe the predicate 'is true' in some more satisfactory way. The move which comes to mind at once, of course, is to construe it as designating a relation between what people assert or think, on the one hand, and something else—a fact, situation, state of affairs, event, or whatever—on the other; and the relation which seems to be called for is that of agreeing with, fitting, answering to—or, to use the traditional expression, corresponding to. A true thought, according to this account, is one that corresponds to a fact, situation, state of affairs, or whatever.

There can be no denying the attractiveness of this view: it seems to be just right. It struck the great philosophers who first considered the problem of truth—viz., Plato and Aristotle—as so obviously the correct one that the question of possible alternatives to it never occurred to them.[4] And certainly if there were such a thing as the common-sense view of truth, it would be the correspondence theory. Common-sense views of this sort may all, in the end, be correct, once they are properly understood; and to call them "common-sense views" is to claim that at the outset they appear to be straightforwardly and undeniably correct. But between the outset and the end (when they are at last "properly understood")—that is to say, when they are in the hands of the philosophers—they inevitably run into tough sailing. Such, at any rate, is the fate of the correspondence theory of truth: philosophical arguments can make its initial plausibility seem to vanish into thin air.

The correspondence theory says: truth is a relation—that of correspondence—between what is said or thought and a fact or state of affairs in the world. Difficulties and perplexities arise concerning the nature of this relation and the nature of both its terms. Consider the first term of the relation, that to which the predicate 'true' is applied—namely, what is said or thought. I have been using the vague and ambiguous locution 'what is said or thought' mainly because it *is* vague and ambiguous enough to get by if it is not too carefully examined. But what exactly is meant by 'what is said or thought'? Suppose someone said truly "It is

---

[4] See Plato, *Sophist* 263B, and Aristotle, *Metaphysics*, Book IV, Chap. 7, 1011b 25-8.

raining," so that what he said was true. He spoke or uttered the English sentence 'It is raining,' but *that* is not what we want to call true. If instead of "It is raining" he had said "Il pleut" or "Es regnet," then in the sense of 'said' in which what he said was true, he would still have said the same thing, for these are just three ways of saying the same thing; but he would have uttered a different sentence. Therefore what he said, in the relevant sense—i.e., in the sense according to which what he said is *true*—is not the English sentence 'It is raining.' If one person says "It is raining," another "Il pleut," and a third "Es regnet," a correct answer to the question "What did he say?" would in each case be "He said that it is raining"—for each would have said *the same thing*. And it is this element which all three utterances have in common—this same thing that is said in all three cases—that is the real bearer of truth, not the different sentences which the speakers happen to utter.

But what *is* this common element? It is, evidently, the common idea behind each of the separate utterances, the common thought which each of the different sentences is used to express. Not, mind you, the thoughts qua individual acts of thinking that occur at certain definite times and in certain particular minds, for those are different individual events and what we want is some *one* thing which is common to them all. What we want is the identical *content* of these different acts of thinking, that *of which* they are all acts of thinking. This content of any number of possible individual thoughts has been called a *proposition:* and it has been held that propositions are the real bearers of truth (and falsity).

It seems sometimes to have been assumed as obvious that propositions must be objective *entities,* on the ground that if two or more sentences all express the same thing, then of course there must be a thing which they all express. The same conviction was also reached as follows. When a person thinks or believes something, it is always a proposition that he thinks or believes. Hence, a proposition is an entity; for whenever a person thinks or believes something, there must *be* a thing that he thinks or believes.[5]

Propositions were thus often conceived to be timeless nonlinguistic entities capable of being apprehended, and of being believed or disbelieved, by any number of different minds. This conception of propositions encounters numerous difficulties, of which I shall discuss two kinds.

(a) We may begin by noting that there is a strong temptation to strip a proposition of any assertive force. Consider the following utterances: (i) The door is shut, (ii) Shut the door!, (iii) Is the door shut?, (iv) Oh, if the door were only shut!, (v) If the door is shut, then the picnic is off, (vi) The door is not shut, (vii) Either the door is shut

---

[5]See Plato, *Theaetetus* 189A, and L. Wittgenstein, *Philosophical Investigations* (Oxford: Basil Blackwell & Mott, Ltd., 1953), Part I, ؟ec. 518.

or I've lost my mind. It is obvious that there is something in common to all these utterances, namely the idea, as we might put it, of the door's being shut. If we have no special prejudices in favor of categorical assertions and thus give no logical priority to utterances like (i), as against any of the other possible kinds, then we might naturally view the mere idea of the door's being shut as a kind of intelligible content or matter which minds can coolly contemplate and which utterances can embody with various different forms imposed upon it. Thus in (i), it is asserted that the content (the door's being shut) describes an actual state of affairs—the content is *asserted;* in (ii) the order is given that the content describe, in the near future, an actual state of affairs—the content is ordered; and so on. This intelligible content looks like our old friend the proposition, only stripped now of its assertive force.[6]

This way of regarding propositions seems right on at least one count: it makes asserting, ordering, questioning, and so on, actions which *people* perform by saying something, rather than actions which are mysteriously embodied, without any agent to perform them, in a wordless abstract entity that exists independently of human or other agents. Notice, however, that this new nonassertorial entity is *not,* although it may appear to be, the same thing as the proposition we began with. Propositions were introduced as the common ideas or thoughts which several different sentences may express. Such an idea or thought, however, contained an assertive element: in our example, it was the thought that it is raining— not the mere nonassertorial thought of its raining, but the assertorial thought that it *is* raining.

This new nonassertorial way of regarding propositions engenders difficulties. One could argue as follows, for example: (i) A mere intelligible content, such as "the door's being shut," cannot be true or false, since it makes no claim; it *asserts* (or *denies*) nothing. If someone were to assert (or deny) the content, by saying "The door is (or is not) shut," then his remark would indeed be true or false, but the content itself is neither. *Comment:* This plausible line of argument deprives the proposition of the very role for which it was invented—namely, that of being the sole bearer of truth (and falsity).[7]

To avoid this trouble, one might argue instead in the following way: (ii) Of course remarks, assertions, statements, and so on, can be true, but so can propositions. Propositions, on the present nonassertorial view, are the intelligible contents of remarks and hence, it may be said, are

---

[6] See C. I. Lewis, *An Analysis of Knowledge and Valuation* (LaSalle, Ill.: Open Court Publishing Co., 1946), p. 49.

[7] Hereafter I shall avoid the needless and annoying repetition of such expressions as 'and falsity,' 'or falsehood,' 'and false,' and so on; they should, however, be understood, wherever appropriate.

used to make true remarks; but both the propositions and the remarks are true. Consider this analogy: a die can be used to form star-shaped cookies, but both the cookie and the die are star-shaped:[8] why, then, should not a proposition and the remarks, statements, etc. it is used to make both be capable of truth? A true proposition will not be a true *assertion,* of course (just as the die is not a star-shaped cookie); it will be more like a true picture or representation of reality. *Comment:* For the present nonassertorial view of propositions, this line of reasoning is more satisfactory than the first, but it does introduce a kind of schizophrenia into the theory of truth, for it makes two radically different kinds of things the bearers of truth. Moreover, the sense in which remarks, assertions, and so on, are true seems to be somewhat different from that in which nonassertorial propositions are, if the latter are at all like pictures or representations. This dualistic result may not be fatal to the view under consideration, but it does make it untidy, at least.

(b) Whether propositions retain their assertive force or not, however, the very notion of a proposition as a timeless, wordless entity is fraught with well-known difficulties. How are we to conceive of this sort of entity? What, for example, are its constituents? The answer that immediately suggests itself, and indeed seems to be the only possible one, is that a proposition is composed of the meanings of the individual words or phrases making up the various different sentences which may be used to express it. The reasoning which lends support to this answer is the following: (i) Propositions were introduced in the first place as being what two or more sentences *with the same meaning* (e.g., 'It is raining,' 'Il pleut,' and 'Es regnet') have in common. Evidently, then, (ii) a proposition is the common meaning of all the sentences that can be used to express it. And so, (iii) a proposition must be composed of the meanings of the individual words or phrases which make up those sentences.

Let us accept this argument for the moment. Let us even swallow the camel of admitting the existence of Platonic meanings corresponding to each word. Still, there are some troublesome gnats to be strained at. First, if a proposition is to be formed, it is not enough that there simply *be* the Platonic meanings of the relevant individual words: the meanings must also be combined with one another. But what are the rules of combination, how is the combination supposed to be brought about, and what sort of complex entity is the result? Consider the corresponding problem at the level of words. In order to have a sentence, a group of individual words must be combined. But here we have a reasonably clear idea of how this is done: a person does it by writing (or speaking) the words one after another in accordance with the rules of syntax for the language,

---

[8] This analogy was suggested to me by Richard Rorty.

and the resulting complex entity is of a familiar sort. But it is not at all clear that we understand what is supposed to go on at the higher level of Platonic meanings. For example, are there rules of meaning-combination as there are rules of word-combination—rules of conceptual syntax? If so, what are they? When one tries to discover what they are, he sees either nothing or mere pale reflections of ordinary syntactical rules —and that ought to make us suspicious. And suppose there were such things as rules of conceptual syntax: what would it be to *combine* the individual Platonic meanings in accordance with the rules? Not writing them down next to each other or speaking them one after another; for one cannot write down or speak a meaning (in this sense of 'a meaning'). Are they then just eternally combined with each other in all the possible ways—thus constituting immutable conceptual facts in Plato's heaven— and does the mind, when it entertains a proposition, simply pick out for consideration one of these everlasting possible combinations? But then this account does not differ, except verbally, from saying that the individual Platonic meanings are *not* combined in themselves at all, and that the mind combines them by thinking them together in some as yet unexplained way, when it entertains propositions.

The foregoing difficulties need not, however, exercise us unduly, for the argument (i)-(iii) (of the last paragraph but one) which gave rise to them is not acceptable. Plausible as it may have seemed, it cannot be accepted, for both (i) and (ii) are false. (i) is false: propositions were introduced as the common content of what is said or asserted when, in a number of utterances, the same thing is said or asserted. In the particular example I gave earlier, three sentences having the same meaning happened to be used: but this was not essential, for the same thing is often said or asserted by using sentences with different meanings. Sam Jones' brother says "My brother is sick"; the same Sam Jones' mother says, at the same time, "My son is sick"; and his son, at the same time, says "My father is sick." It is plausible to suppose that all three people asserted the same thing—i.e., expressed the same proposition—and yet no one could reasonably maintain that the three sentences they used all have the same meaning. And (ii) is false: if a proposition is the bearer of truth (and falsity), then it cannot be the meaning of a class of sentences, for, as Austin points out (see below, p. 20) "We never say 'The meaning (or sense) of this sentence (or of these words) is true.'" Again, although we can say of a proposition that it was asserted or denied, it makes no sense to say this of the meaning of a sentence.[9]

---

[9] I owe this point to R. Cartwright. See his "Propositions," in *Analytical Philosophy*, R. J. Butler, ed. (Oxford: Basil Blackwell & Mott, Ltd., 1962), p. 101. In this article, the points here under discussion, and related ones, are treated perceptively and thoroughly.

I conclude that the argument does not establish (iii). And, since the initial plausibility of (iii) derives entirely from (ii), which is false, I conclude also that (iii) is false. But if the meanings of words are not the constituents of propositions, what are? What *are* the constituents of what-a-person-asserts, the *content* of what he says? It seems difficult, or impossible, to answer. But this must surely be a great embarrassment to those who hold that propositions are real entities: if we cannot even begin to say what their constituents are, we hardly have a clear idea of what *they* are.

Here I shall cut short the unhappy tale of those woes which beset the correspondence theory of truth from the side of the alleged truth-bearers —viz., propositions: I want to get on to some other problematic features of the theory. But first it ought to be made clear that the troubles I have been discussing cannot in fairness be said to be troubles which *the* correspondence theory of truth encounters, as if the version of the theory presented so far in these pages were the only one there is. It is not. For one thing, many defenders of the theory have not conceived propositions to be entities such as I have described: propositions have also been held to be mental entities of one sort or another, to be linguistic entities of various sorts (e.g., declarative sentences or classes of such sentences), to be identical with the facts they describe—and they have been conceived in other ways as well. For another, many defenders of the theory have not even held that *propositions* are the bearers of truth at all: other leading candidates for this role have been beliefs, judgments, sentences, assertions, and statements. Needless to say, it will not be possible to explore here all these alternatives to the particular view I have been discussing. Some of them are not open, of course, to the objections I have raised, although they have troubles of their own. All I have tried to do is point out some typical *kinds* of problems which correspondence theories of truth, as traditionally conceived, encounter.

Puzzles about propositions are not confined to the correspondence theory alone: they can plague any theory of truth whatever. Now I turn to problems which are peculiar to the correspondence theory. I shall begin with the crucial notion of correspondence itself. It seems to me that there are two different kinds of correspondence which might be relevant to a theory of truth. The first amounts to little more than mere correlation of the members of two or more groups of things, in accordance with some rule(s) or principle(s). Consider, for example, what is meant when mathematicians speak of a one-to-one correspondence. The series of integers can be put into one-to-one correspondence with the series of even integers, as follows:

Series A (integers)	1	2	3	4	5	6	... n
	↓	↓	↓	↓	↓	↓	↓
Series B (even integers)	2	4	6	8	10	12	... 2n

We may say that the 1 of Series A corresponds to the 2 of Series B, that the 12 of Series B corresponds to the 6 of Series A, and so on. What is involved here is the following: given any member x_i of one group, A, and the rule $y = 2x$, there is a unique member y_i of the other group, B, which satisfies this rule; and all it means to say that x_i corresponds to y_i (e.g., that the 1 of A corresponds to the 2 of B) is that x_i of group A and y_i of group B are correlated or paired off with one another in accordance with the stated rule. But without any indicated grouping or without some rule being either explicitly mentioned or tacitly understood, it hardly makes sense to speak of correspondence: what, for example, could be meant by claiming, out of the blue, that 1 corresponds to 2, or that 12 corresponds to 6? Again, if we were talking about forms of government, we might say that the British Parliament corresponds to our (American) Congress: and this would mean that the two can be paired off with one another in accordance with the principle that they serve (at least roughly) the same functions in their respective forms of government. This common kind of correspondence I shall call *correspondence-as-correlation*.

There is also another kind of correspondence. If two bits of paper each have a torn edge, so that when they are placed together the fit is perfect, then we can say that the two edges, or the two pieces of paper, exactly correspond. Again, if two witnesses are queried separately by the police about a shooting incident and they both tell exactly the same story, then their two accounts correspond perfectly—or correspond down to the last detail. The *Shorter Oxford English Dictionary* defines this sense of 'correspond' as follows: "To answer to something else in the way of fitness; to agree *with;* be conformable *to;* be congruous or in harmony *with.*" This kind of correspondence I shall call *correspondence-as-congruity*.

There seem to be two different senses of 'correspond' involved in 'correspondence-as-correlation' and 'correspondence-as-congruity.' This is indicated by the fact that all cases of correspondence-as-congruity can be qualified as perfect or exact, whereas this is not true of correspondence-as-correlation: for example, the 1 of Series A cannot sensibly be said to correspond perfectly (or imperfectly) with the 2 of Series B. To be sure, sometimes correspondence-as-correlation can be exact, but then the phrase 'corresponds exactly' means something different from what it means in connection with correspondence-as-congruity: thus the British Parliament *could* be said (no doubt inaccurately) to correspond exactly—but not, notice, *perfectly*—to the American Congress. But this would not mean that two legislative bodies "agree with" or are "conformable to" one another; it would mean that they perform exactly the same function in their respective forms of government.

Granted, then, that correspondence-as-correlation (where correspondence is a "weak" relation, a mere pairing of members of two or more groups in accordance with some principle) is to be distinguished from correspondence-as-congruity (where correspondence is a "richer" relation of harmony or agreement between the two or more things), the question that now presents itself is whether the correspondence theory construes truth as a relation of correspondence-as-correlation or as one of correspondence-as-congruity. There can be little doubt that the main impetus of traditional correspondence theories has been towards the latter interpretation: defenders of the theory tended to think of a proposition and the fact it states as two separate complexes which exactly fit each other. In the proposition "The cat is on the mat," 'the cat' designates the cat, 'on' designates the relation of being on, and 'the mat' designates the mat: the proposition asserts that the first (the cat) and third (the mat) in that order, are related by the second (the relation of being on). The fact that the cat is on the mat consists of the cat and the mat, related so that the former is on the latter. The agreement is perfect. Ludwig Wittgenstein (1889-1951), who in his early *Tractatus Logico-Philosophicus*[10] worked out this conception of the correspondence theory more thoroughly than had ever been done before, came to the conclusion that at least elementary propositions, those to which all others are reducible by analysis, are perfect (logical) pictures of the states of affairs they describe. The congruity that exists between a proposition and the reality it describes is thus considered to be of the same intimate kind as that which exists between a perfect representation of something and that of which it is the representation.

The difficulties which the correspondence theory, conceived in this way, encounters are enormous. I shall mention three of them, but discuss only the first in any detail. It is obvious that if the view is even to get off the ground, the real parts of a proposition must be at least roughly distinguishable, for it is just in virtue of a connection between (a) the parts of the proposition and (b) the parts of the fact it describes, that the proposition as a whole is congruent with—i.e., corresponds to—the fact as a whole. The first difficulty facing this correspondence (-as-congruity) theory is that the problem of determining, even roughly, how many con-

---

[10] Translated by D. F. Pears and B. F. McGuinness (New York: The Humanities Press, 1961). This work was completed in 1918, and the first English translation appeared in 1922.

stituents a proposition has is horribly difficult, if not totally insoluble. As we have already seen (pp. 7-9), there is a tremendous problem about determining what *sort of thing* the constituents of a proposition are: the initially most plausible view—namely, that they are the meanings of words—turned out to be false, and no other plausible view presented itself. That troublesome question, however, can be by-passed in order to discuss this new one—namely, the question of determining *how many* constituents a proposition has: for it is not always essential, in order to determine how many x's there are, to know exactly what sort of thing x's are. In the present case of propositions, in particular, it might seem obvious that even though the constituents of a proposition cannot be identified with the meanings of the words or phrases which make up a sentence that can be used to express it, nevertheless there must be one constituent of a proposition (whatever its *nature* may be) corresponding to each main grammatical part of such a sentence. Perhaps it seems obvious, for example, that there are exactly three constituents of the proposition expressed by the sentence 'The cat is on the mat'—namely, those corresponding to the words 'the cat,' 'the mat,' and '_____ is on _____.' But difficulties immediately present themselves. There is a foreign language—I have just invented it—in which the proposition we express by saying "The cat is on the mat" is expressed by the one-word sentence 'Catamat.' Are we to say that when a speaker of this new language says "Catamat" he is expressing a proposition with only one constituent? But then how could that be the same proposition as the one we express by saying "The cat is on the mat," since ours has three constituents? Perhaps we are tempted to say that his proposition really has the same three constituents that ours does, since when he says "Catamat," what he means is that the cat (1) is on (2) the mat (3). This is true. But *he* can say, with as much justice, both (a) that when he says "Catamat," what he means is *catamat, and* (b) that when *we* say "The cat is on the mat," what we mean is *catamat*. So we are right back where we started. (See Wittgenstein, *Philosophical Investigations*, Part I, Secs. 19 and 20.)

What to do? (a) Are we to insist that the two sentences 'The cat is on the mat' and 'Catamat' both express the same proposition although conceding that the former has three constituents while the latter has only one? Identity of propositions would then have to be a matter not of the identity of their constituents, but rather of the identity of the facts or states of affairs they describe. But then since the correspondence (-as-congruity) of two things x and y involves some pairings of the respective parts of x and y, if one of these two propositions corresponds to the state of affairs, it is difficult to see how the other possibly could. This is difficult to see, at any rate, if one assumes, with most defenders of the correspondence theory, that states of affairs are real complex entities with a certain fixed number of constituents. One could try to reject that assumption: one could say that the proposition "The cat is on the mat" describes the state of affairs S_1 of the cat's being on the mat, which consists of three elements, while the proposition "Catamat" describes the state of affairs S_2 of cat'samat, which consists of only one element. But then the state of affairs S_1 could not without circularity be identified with S_2, as it must be if the suggestion under consideration is to stand. The reason for this is as follows: a state of affairs can only be picked out, in the end, by means of language. We can pick out S_1 only as that state of affairs which is described by the proposition expressed by the sentence 'The cat is on the mat'; and we can pick out S_2 only as that state of affairs which is described by the proposition expressed by the sentence 'Catamat.' Now we cannot without circularity go on to claim that S_1 and S_2 are the *same* state of affairs; because this claim could only be backed up by the contention that the propositions "The cat is on the mat" and "Catamat" are identical. But *ex hypothesi* these two propositions are themselves identical solely in virtue of their describing the same state of affairs.

(b) Shall we say, then, that the two sentences 'The cat is on the mat' and 'Catamat' express one and the same proposition, the number of whose constituents has no necessary connection with the number of expressions in either of the two sentences? But then *how* are we to determine this number? (c) Shall we abandon the search for the number of constituents of a proposition and contend that the question of how many constituents a proposition has is a wholly arbitrary one having no right answer? But then we would seem to be abandoning at the same time all hope of construing truth in terms of correspondence-as-congruity, since this kind of correspondence between two things seems to require the pairing of their respective parts.

The second kind of trouble with the correspondence-as-congruity theory arises from the fact that the most plausible candidate for the relation binding the respective parts of a proposition and the state of affairs it describes seems to be that of *designating, standing for,* or *denoting.* A denotative theory of meaning[11] is at least a natural adjunct to the correspondence theory of truth conceived in the present way, if it is not actually an essential part of it: the two were certainly intimately connected in Wittgenstein's *Tractatus.* But the unsatisfactoriness of any purely denotative theory of meaning is well-known, thanks largely to

---

[11] I.e., one that construes the meaning of a term to be whatever it designates or denotes.

the later work, paradoxically enough, of Wittgenstein himself. The third set of difficulties facing the correspondence (-as-congruity) theory are those concerning the nature and hence the constituents of facts; since this topic is discussed in the pages that follow, however—notably by Strawson in "Truth"—I shall say nothing about it.[12]

It would appear that the only hope for the correspondence theory is not to view correspondence as a "rich" relation of congruity, but rather as a "weak" relation of mere correlation or pairing of individual propositions and facts. This version of the correspondence theory completely avoids the first two of the three kinds of difficulties encountered by the other version: there is no need for it to distinguish the parts of a proposition, and there is no necessity for it to embrace a denotative theory of meaning. It is, however, committed to an objective view of facts, or of some substitute for facts, and so is open to at least some of the criticisms on this score that the earlier version is. I shall say no more about this version of the correspondence theory: it is, in all essential respects, just the view which is so ably defended by Austin in the present volume. (Austin explicitly denies, however, that propositions are the only, and even that they very often *are,* bearers of truth.)

The most important recent development in theories of truth, prior to the Austin-Strawson debate of 1950, was undoubtedly the introduction, by F. P. Ramsey (1903-1930), of the view that the predicates 'true' and 'false' do not designate either properties of propositions or relations between propositions and something else. They do not, in fact, designate anything, contrary to what all previous theories had assumed.[13]

The stage is now set for the Austin-Strawson debate with which the greater part of the pages that follow are concerned. Austin defends, as I said, a version of the correspondence theory of truth, while Strawson presents a view which grows out of Ramsey's germinal idea. Which

---

[12] Interested readers may consult the following works: J. L. Austin, "Unfair to Facts"; P. Herbst, "The Nature of Facts"; B. Russell, "The Philosophy of Logical Atomism"; F. P. Ramsey, "Facts and Propositions"; G. E. Moore, "Facts and Propositions"; J. R. Lucas, "On Not Worshipping Facts." For full references, see the bibliography at the end of this book.

[13] Ramsey's basic idea is actually first found in a writing of Gottlob Frege (1848-1925) dating from 1892: "One can, indeed, say: 'The thought, that 5 is a prime number, is true.' But closer examination shows that nothing more has been said than in the simple sentence '5 is a prime number.'" [G. Frege, "On Sense and Reference," *Translations from the Writings of Gottlob Frege,* P. Geach and M. Black, eds. (Oxford: Basil Blackwell & Mott, Ltd., 1952), p. 64.] Frege, however, did not hold that 'true' designates nothing: on the contrary, he thought it designates an object which he called "The True." [See R. Sternfeld, "A Restriction in Frege's Use of the Term 'True,'" *Philosophical Studies,* Vol. VI (1955).]

philosopher has more of the truth on his side? That is a question which each reader will have to decide for himself.[14]

[14] My colleagues Joel Feinberg and Richard Rorty read this Introduction and made many helpful suggestions: I am happy to record my debt of gratitude to them. I take this opportunity also to thank the following: Mrs. J. Austin for her kind permission to reprint J. L. Austin's article "Truth," Mrs. L. Ramsey for her kind permission to reprint the selection from F. P. Ramsey's "Facts and Propositions," Messrs. Dummett and Strawson for permission to reprint their essays and/or the selections from their books, the publishers of the books and the editors of the philosophical journals in which the works reprinted here have previously appeared, and Messrs. Strawson and Warnock, who wrote their articles, "A Problem about Truth," specially for this volume.

FACTS AND PROPOSITIONS

F. P. RAMSEY

. . . But before we proceed further with the analysis of judgment, it is necessary to say something about truth and falsehood, in order to show that there is really no separate problem of truth but merely a linguistic muddle. Truth and falsity are ascribed primarily to propositions. The proposition to which they are ascribed may be either explicitly given or described. Suppose first that it is explicitly given; then it is evident that 'It is true that Cæsar was murdered' means no more than that Cæsar was murdered, and 'It is false that Cæsar was murdered' means that Cæsar was not murdered. They are phrases which we sometimes use for emphasis or for stylistic reasons, or to indicate the position occupied by the statement in our argument. So also we can say 'It is a fact that he was murdered' or 'That he was murdered is contrary to fact.'

From "Facts and Propositions," Proceedings of the Aristotelian Society, *Supp. Vol. VII* (1927). *Reprinted in* The Foundations of Mathematics (*London: Routledge & Kegan Paul, Ltd.; New York: The Humanities Press, 1931*). *Reprinted by permission of Mrs. Ramsey; the editor of the Aristotelian Society; Routledge & Kegan Paul, Ltd.; and The Humanities Press.*

In the second case in which the proposition is described and not given explicitly we have perhaps more of a problem, for we get statements from which we cannot in ordinary language eliminate the words 'true' and 'false.' Thus if I say 'He is always right,' I mean that the propositions he asserts are always true, and there does not seem to be any way of expressing this without using the word 'true.' But suppose we put it thus 'For all p, if he asserts p, p is true,' then we see that the propositional function p is true is simply the same as p, as e.g., its value 'Cæsar was murdered is true' is the same as 'Cæsar was murdered.' We have in English to add 'is true' to give the sentence a verb, forgetting that 'p' already contains a (variable) verb. This may perhaps be made clearer by supposing for a moment that only one form of proposition is in question, say the relational form aRb; then 'He is always right' could be expressed by 'For all a, R, b, if he asserts aRb, then aRb,' to which 'is true' would be an obviously superfluous addition. When all forms of proposition are included the analysis is more complicated but not essentially different; and it is clear that the problem is not as to the nature of truth and falsehood, but as to the nature of judgment or assertion, for what is difficult to analyze in the above formulation is 'He asserts aRb.'

It is, perhaps, also immediately obvious that if we have analyzed judgment we have solved the problem of truth; for taking the mental factor in a judgment (which is often itself called a judgment), the truth or falsity of this depends only on what proposition it is that is judged, and what we have to explain is the meaning of saying that the judgment is a judgment that a has R to b, i.e., is true if aRb, false if not. We can, if we like, say that it is true if there exists a corresponding fact that a has R to b, but this is essentially not an analysis but a periphrasis, for 'The fact that a has R to b exists' is no different from 'a has R to b.' . . .

TRUTH

J. L. AUSTIN

1. 'What is truth?' said jesting Pilate, and would not stay for an answer. Pilate was in advance of his time. For 'truth' itself is an abstract noun, a camel, that is, of a logical construction, which cannot get past the eye even of a grammarian. We approach it cap and categories in hand: we ask ourselves whether Truth is a substance (the Truth, the Body of Knowledge), or a quality (something like the color red, inhering in truths), or a relation ('correspondence').[1] But philosophers should take something more nearly their own size to strain at. What needs discussing rather is the use, or certain uses, of the word 'true.' *In vino,* possibly, *'veritas,'* but in a sober symposium *'verum.'*

"Truth," Proceedings of the Aristotelian Society, *Supp. Vol. XXIV (1950). Reprinted in* Philosophical Papers, *J. O. Urmson and G. J. Warnock, eds. (Oxford: The Clarendon Press, 1961). Reprinted by permission of Mrs. Austin; the editor of the Aristotelian Society; and The Clarendon Press.*

[1] It is sufficiently obvious that 'truth' is a substantive, 'true' an adjective and 'of' in 'true of' a preposition.

2. What is it that we say is true or is false? Or, how does the phrase 'is true' occur in English sentences? The answers appear at first multifarious. We say (or are said to say) that beliefs are true, that descriptions or accounts are true, that propositions or assertions or statements are true; and that words or sentences are true: and this is to mention only a selection of the more obvious candidates. Again, we say (or are said to say) 'It is true that the cat is on the mat,' or 'It is true to say that the cat is on the mat,' or ' "The cat is on the mat" is true.' We also remark on occasion, when someone else has said something, 'Very true' or 'That's true' or 'True enough.'

Most (though not all) of these expressions, and others besides, certainly do occur naturally enough. But it seems reasonable to ask whether there is not some use of 'is true' that is primary, or some generic name for that which at bottom we are always saying 'is true.' Which, if any, of these expressions is to be taken *au pied de la lettre*? To answer this will not take us long, nor, perhaps, far: but in philosophy the foot of the letter is the foot of the ladder.

I suggest that the following are the primary forms of expression:

It is true (to say) that the cat is on the mat.

That statement (of his, etc.) is true.

The statement that the cat is on the mat is true.

But first for the rival candidates.

(*a*) Some say that 'truth is primarily a property of beliefs.' But it may be doubted whether the expression 'a true belief' is at all common outside philosophy and theology: and it seems clear that a man is said to hold a true belief when and in the sense that he believes (in) *something which* is true, or believes that *something which* is true is true. Moreover if, as some also say, a belief is 'of the nature of a picture,' then it is of the nature of what cannot be true, though it may be, for example, faithful.[2]

(*b*) True descriptions and true accounts are simply varieties of true statements or of collections of true statements, as are true answers and the like. The same applies to propositions too, in so far as they are genuinely said to be true (and not, as more commonly, sound, tenable and so on).[3] A proposition in law or in geometry is something portentous, usually a generalization, that we are invited to accept and that has to be recommended by argument: it cannot be a direct report on current observation—if you look and inform me that the cat is on the mat, that

---

[2] A likeness is true *to* life, but not true *of* it. A *word* picture can be true, just because it is *not* a picture.

[3] Predicates applicable also to 'arguments,' which we likewise do not say are true, but, for example, valid.

is not a proposition though it is a statement. In philosophy, indeed, 'proposition' is sometimes used in a special way for 'the meaning or sense of a sentence or family of sentences': but whether we think a lot or little of this usage, a proposition in this sense cannot, at any rate, be what we say is true or false. For we never say 'The meaning (or sense) of this sentence (or of these words) is true': what we do say is what the judge or jury says, namely that *'The words* taken in this sense, or if we assign to them such and such a meaning, or so interpreted or understood, *are true.'*

(*c*) Words and sentences are indeed said to be true, the former often, the latter rarely. But only in certain senses. Words as discussed by philologists, or by lexicographers, grammarians, linguists, phoneticians, printers, critics (stylistic or textual) and so on, are not true or false: they are wrongly formed, or ambiguous or defective or untranslatable or unpronounceable or misspelled or archaistic or corrupt or what not.[4] Sentences in similar contexts are elliptic or involved or alliterative or ungrammatical. We may, however, genuinely say 'His closing words were very true' or 'The third sentence on page 5 of his speech is quite false': but here 'words' and 'sentence' refer, as is shown by the demonstratives (possessive pronouns, temporal verbs, definite descriptions, etc.), which in this usage consistently accompany them, to the words or sentence *as used by a certain person on a certain occasion.* That is, they refer (as does 'Many a true word spoken in jest') to *statements.*

A statement is made and its making is an historic event, the utterance by a certain speaker or writer of certain words (a sentence) to an audience with reference to an historic situation, event or what not.[5]

A sentence is made *up of* words, a statement is made *in* words. A sentence is not English or not good English, a statement is not in English or not in good English. Statements are made, words or sentences are used. We talk of *my* statement, but of *the English* sentence (if a sentence is mine, I coined it, but I do not coin statements). The *same* sentence is used in making *different* statements (I say 'It is mine,' you say 'It is mine'): it may also be used on two occasions or by two persons in mak-

---

[4] Peirce made a beginning by pointing out that there are two (or three) different senses of the word 'word,' and adumbrated a technique ('counting' words) for deciding what is a 'different sense.' But his two senses are not well defined, and there are many more—the 'vocable' sense, the philologist's sense in which 'grammar' is the same word as 'glamour,' the textual critic's sense in which the 'the' in l. 254 has been written twice, and so on. With all his 66 divisions of signs, Peirce does not, I believe, distinguish between a sentence and a statement.

[5] 'Historic' does not, of course, mean that we cannot speak of future or possible statements. A 'certain' speaker need not be any definite speaker. 'Utterance' need not be public utterance—the audience may be the speaker himself.

ing the *same* statement, but for this the utterance must be made with reference to the same situation or event.[6] We speak of 'the statement that S,' but of 'the sentence "S," ' not of 'the sentence that S.' [7]

When I say that a statement is what is true, I have no wish to become wedded to one word. 'Assertion,' for example, will in most contexts do just as well, though perhaps it is slightly wider. Both words share the weakness of being rather solemn (much more so than the more general 'what you said' or 'your words')—though perhaps we are generally being a little solemn when we discuss the truth of anything. Both have the merit of clearly referring to the historic use of a sentence by an utterer, and of being therefore precisely not equivalent to 'sentence.' For it is a fashionable mistake to take as primary '(The sentence) "S" is true (in the English language).' Here the addition of the words 'in the English language' serves to emphasize that 'sentence' is not being used as equivalent to 'statement,' so that it precisely is not what can be true or false (and moreover, 'true in the English language' is a solecism, mismodeled presumably, and with deplorable effect, on expressions like 'true in geometry').

3. When is a statement true? The temptation is to answer (at least if we confine ourselves to 'straightforward' statements): 'When it corresponds to the facts.' And as a piece of standard English this can hardly be wrong. Indeed, I must confess I do not really think it is wrong at all: the theory of truth is a series of truisms. Still, it can at least be misleading.

If there is to be communication of the sort that we achieve by language at all, there must be a stock of symbols of some kind which a communicator ('the speaker') can produce 'at will' and which a communicatee ('the audience') can observe: these may be called the 'words,' though, of course, they need not be anything very like what we should normally call words

---

[6] 'The same' does not always mean the same. In fact it has no meaning in the way that an 'ordinary' word like 'red' or 'horse' has a meaning: it is a (the typical) device for establishing and distinguishing the meanings of ordinary words. Like 'real,' it is part of our apparatus *in* words for fixing and adjusting the semantics *of* words.

[7] Inverted commas show that the words, though uttered (in writing), are not to be taken as a statement by the utterer. This covers two possible cases, (i) where what is to be discussed is the sentence, (ii) where what is to be discussed is a statement made elsewhen in the words 'quoted.' Only in case (i) is it correct to say simply that the token is doing duty for the type (and even here it is quite incorrect to say that 'The cat is on the mat' is the *name* of an English sentence—though possibly *The Cat is on the Mat* might be the title of a novel, or a bull might be known as *Catta est in matta*). Only in case (ii) is there something true or false, viz. (not the quotation but) the statement made in the words quoted.

—they might be signal flags, etc. There must also be something other than the words, which the words are to be used to communicate about: this may be called the 'world.' There is no reason why the world should not include the words, in every sense except the sense of the actual statement itself which on any particular occasion is being made about the world. Further, the world must exhibit (we must observe) similarities and dissimilarities (there could not be the one without the other): if everything were either absolutely indistinguishable from anything else or completely unlike anything else, there would be nothing to say. And finally (for present purposes—of course there are other conditions to be satisfied too) there must be two sets of conventions:

Descriptive conventions correlating the words (= sentences) with the *types* of situation, thing, event, etc., to be found in the world.
Demonstrative conventions correlating the words (= statements) with the *historic* situations, etc., to be found in the world.[8]

A statement is said to be true when the historic state of affairs to which it is correlated by the demonstrative conventions (the one to which it 'refers') is of a type[9] with which the sentence used in making it is correlated by the descriptive conventions.[10]

3*a*. Troubles arise from the use of the word 'facts' for the historic situations, events, etc., and in general, for the world. For 'fact' is regularly used in conjunction with 'that' in the sentences 'The fact is that S'

---

[8] Both sets of conventions may be included together under 'semantics.' But they differ greatly.

[9] 'Is of a type with which' means 'is sufficiently like those standard states of affairs with which.' Thus, for a statement to be true one state of affairs must be *like* certain others, which is a natural relation, but also *sufficiently* like to merit the same 'description,' which is no longer a purely natural relation. To say 'This is red' is not the same as to say 'This is like those,' nor even as to say 'This is like those which were called red.' That things are *similar,* or even 'exactly' similar, I may literally see, but that they are the *same* I cannot literally see—in calling them the same color a convention is involved additional to the conventional choice of the name to be given to the color which they are said to be.

[10] The trouble is that sentences contain words or verbal devices to serve both descriptive and demonstrative purposes (not to mention other purposes), often both at once. In philosophy we mistake the descriptive for the demonstrative (theory of universals) or the demonstrative for the descriptive (theory of monads). A sentence as normally distinguished from a mere word or phrase is characterized by its containing a minimum of verbal demonstrative devices (Aristotle's 'reference to time'); but many demonstrative conventions are non-verbal (pointing, etc.), and using these we can make a statement in a single word which is not a 'sentence.' Thus, 'languages' like that of (traffic, etc.) *signs* use quite distinct media for their descriptive and demonstrative elements (the sign on the post, the site of the post). And however many verbal demonstrative devices we use as auxiliaries, there must *always* be a nonverbal *origin* for these coordinates, which is the point of utterance of the statement.

or 'It is a fact that S' and in the expression 'the fact that S,' all of which imply that it would be true to say that S.[11]

This may lead us to suppose that

(i) 'fact' is only an alternative expression for 'true statement.' We note that when a detective says 'Let's look at the facts' he does not crawl round the carpet, but proceeds to utter a string of statements: we even talk of 'stating the facts';

(ii) for every true statement there exists 'one' and its own precisely corresponding fact—for every cap the head it fits.

It is (i) which leads to some of the mistakes in 'coherence' or formalist theories; (ii) to some of those in 'correspondence' theories. Either we suppose that there is nothing there but the true statement itself, nothing to which it corresponds, or else we populate the world with linguistic *Doppelgänger* (and grossly overpopulate it—every nugget of 'positive' fact overlaid by a massive concentration of 'negative' facts, every tiny detailed fact larded with generous general facts, and so on).

When a statement is true, there is, *of course,* a state of affairs which makes it true and which is *toto mundo* distinct from the true statement about it: but equally of course, we can only *describe* that state of affairs *in words* (either the same or, with luck, others). I can only describe the situation in which it is true to say that I am feeling sick by saying that it is one in which I am feeling sick (or experiencing sensations of nausea):[12] yet between stating, however truly, that I am feeling sick and feeling sick there is a great gulf fixed.[13]

'Fact that' is a phrase designed for use in situations where the distinction between a true statement and the state of affairs about which it is a

---

[11] I use the following *abbreviations:*
S for the cat is on the mat.
ST for it is true that the cat is on the mat.
tst for the statement that.
I take tstS as my example throughout and not, say, tst Julius Caesar was bald or tst all mules are sterile, because these latter are apt in their different ways to make us overlook the distinction between sentence and statement: we have, apparently, in the one case a sentence capable of being used to refer to only one historic situation, in the other a statement without reference to at least (or to any particular) one.
If space permitted other types of statement (existential, general, hypothetical, etc.) should be dealt with: these raise problems rather of meaning than of truth, though I feel uneasiness about hypotheticals.

[12] If this is what was meant by ' "It is raining" is true if and only if it is raining,' so far so good.

[13] It takes two to make a truth. Hence (obviously) there can be no criterion of truth in the sense of some feature detectable in the statement itself which will reveal whether it is true or false. Hence, too, a statement cannot without absurdity refer to itself.

truth is neglected; as it often is with advantage in ordinary life, though seldom in philosophy—above all in discussing truth, where it is precisely our business to prize the words off the world and keep them off it. To ask 'Is the fact that S the true statement that S or that which it is true of?' may beget absurd answers. To take an analogy: although we may sensibly ask 'Do we *ride* the word "elephant" or the animal?' and equally sensibly 'Do we *write* the word or the animal?' it is nonsense to ask 'Do we *define* the word or the animal?' For defining an elephant (supposing we ever do this) is a compendious description of an operation involving both word and animal (do we focus the image or the battleship?) ; and so speaking about 'the fact that' is a compendious way of speaking about a situation involving both words and world.[14]

3*b*. 'Corresponds' also gives trouble, because it is commonly given too restricted or too colorful a meaning, or one which in this context it cannot bear. The only essential point is this: that the correlation between the words (= sentences) and the type of situation, event, etc. which is to be such that when a statement in those words is made with reference to an historic situation of that type the statement is then true, is *absolutely and purely* conventional. We are absolutely free to appoint *any* symbol to describe *any* type of situation, so far as merely being true goes. In a small one-spade language tst nuts might be true in exactly the same circumstances as the statement in English that the National Liberals are the people's choice.[15] There is no need whatsoever for the words used in making a true statement to 'mirror' in any way, however indirect, any feature whatsoever of the situation or event; a statement no more needs, in order to be true, to reproduce the 'multiplicity,' say, or the 'structure' or 'form' of the reality, than a word needs to be echoic or writing pictographic. To suppose that it does, is to fall once again into the error of reading back into the world the features of language.

The more rudimentary a language, the more, very often, it will tend to have a 'single' word for a highly 'complex' type of situation: this has such disadavantages as that the language becomes elaborate to learn and is incapable of dealing with situations which are nonstandard, unforeseen, for which there may just be no word. When we go abroad equipped only with a phrase-book, we may spend long hours learning by heart—

A¹-moest-faᶦnd-ᵉtschâʳwoumᵉn,
Maᶦhwîl-iz-wauʳpt (bènt),

---

[14] 'It is true that S' and 'It is a fact that S' are applicable in the same circumstances; the cap fits when there is a head it fits. Other words can fill the same role as 'fact': we say, e.g., 'The situation is that S.'

[15] We could use 'nuts' even now as a codeword: but a code, as a transformation of a language, is distinguished from a language, and a codeword dispatched is not (called) 'true.'

and so on and so on, yet faced with the situation where we have the pen of our aunt, find ourselves quite unable to say so. The characteristics of a more developed language (articulation, morphology, syntax, abstractions, etc.), do not make statements in it any more capable of being true or capable of being any more true, they make it more adaptable, more learnable, more comprehensive, more precise, and so on; and *these* aims may no doubt be furthered by making the language (allowance made for the nature of the medium) 'mirror' in conventional ways features descried in the world.

Yet even when a language does 'mirror' such features very closely (and does it ever?) the truth of statements remains still a matter, as it was with the most rudimentary languages, of the words used being the ones *conventionally appointed* for situations of the type to which that referred to belongs. A picture, a copy, a replica, a photograph—these are *never* true in so far as they are reproductions, produced by natural or mechanical means: a reproduction can be accurate or lifelike (true *to* the original), as a gramophone recording or a transcription may be, but not true (*of*) as a record of proceedings can be. In the same way a (natural) sign *of* something can be infallible or unreliable but only an (artificial) sign *for* something can be right or wrong.[16]

There are many intermediate cases between a true account and a faithful picture, as here somewhat forcibly contrasted, and it is from the study of these (a lengthy matter) that we can get the clearest insight into the contrast. For example, maps: these may be called pictures, yet they are highly conventionalized pictures. If a map can be clear or accurate or misleading, like a statement, why can it not be true or exaggerated? How do the 'symbols' used in mapmaking differ from those used in statement-making? On the other hand, if an air-mosaic is not a map, why is it not? And when does a map become a diagram? These are the really illuminating questions.

4. Some have said that—

To say that an assertion is true is not to make any further assertion at all.

In all sentences of the form '*p* is true' the phrase 'is true' is logically superfluous.

To say that a proposition is true is just to assert it, and to say that it is false is just to assert its contradictory.

But wrongly. TstS (except in parodoxical cases of forced and dubious manufacture) refers to the world or any part of it exclusive of tstS, i.e.,

---

[16] Berkeley confuses these two. There will not be books in the running brooks until the dawn of hydrosemantics.

of itself.[17] TstST refers to the world or any part of it *inclusive* of tstS, though once again exclusive of itself, i.e., of tstST. That is, tstST refers to something to which tstS cannot refer. TstST does not, certainly, include any statement referring to the world exclusive of tstS which is not included already in tstS—more, it seems doubtful whether it does include that statement about the world exclusive of tstS which is made when we state that S. (If I state that tstS is true, should we really agree that I have stated that S? Only 'by implication.')[18] But all this does not go any way to show that tstST is not a statement different from tstS. If Mr. Q writes on a notice-board 'Mr. W is a burglar,' then a trial is held to decide whether Mr. Q's published statement that Mr. W is a burglar is a libel: finding 'Mr. Q's statement was true (in substance and in fact).' Thereupon a second trial is held, to decide whether Mr. W is a burglar, in which Mr. Q's statement is no longer under consideration: verdict 'Mr. W is a burglar.' It is an arduous business to hold a second trial: why is it done if the verdict is the same as the previous finding? [19]

What is felt is that the evidence considered in arriving at the one verdict is the same as that considered in arriving at the other. This is not strictly correct. It is more nearly correct that whenever tstS is true then tstST is also true and conversely, and that whenever tstS is false tstST is also false and conversely.[20] And it is argued that the words 'is true' are logically superfluous because it is believed that generally if any two statements are always true together and always false together then they must mean the same. Now whether this is in general a sound view may be doubted: but even if it is, why should it not break down in the case of so obviously 'peculiar' a phrase as 'is true'? Mistakes in philosophy notoriously arise through thinking that what holds of 'ordinary' words like 'red' or 'growls' must also hold of extraordinary words like 'real' or 'exists.' But that 'true' is just such another extraordinary word is obvious.[21]

---

[17] A statement may refer to 'itself' in the sense, for example, of the sentence used or the utterance uttered in making it ('statement' is not exempt from all ambiguity). But paradox does result if a statement purports to refer to itself in a more full-blooded sense, purports, that is, to state that it itself is true, or to state what it itself refers to ('This statement is about Cato').

[18] And 'by implication' tstST asserts something about the making of a statement which tstS certainly does not assert.

[19] This is not quite fair: there are many legal and personal reasons for holding two trials—which, however, do not affect the point that the issue being tried is not the same.

[20] Not *quite* correct, because tstST is only in place at all when tstS is envisaged as made and has been verified.

[21] *Unum, verum, bonum*—the old favorites deserve their celebrity. There *is* something odd about each of them. Theoretical theology is a form of onomatolatry.

There is something peculiar about the 'fact' which is described by tstST, something which may make us hesitate to call it a 'fact' at all; namely, that the relation between tstS and the world which tstST asserts to obtain is a *purely conventional* relation (one which 'thinking makes so'). For we are aware that this relation is one which we could alter at will, whereas we like to restrict the word 'fact' to *hard* facts, facts which are natural and unalterable, or anyhow not alterable at will. Thus, to take an analogous case, we may not like calling it a fact that the word elephant means what it does, though we can be induced to call it a (soft) fact—and though, of course, we have no hesitation in calling it a fact that contemporary English speakers use the word as they do.

An important point about this view is that it confuses falsity with negation: for according to it, it is the same thing to say 'He is not at home' as to say 'It is false that he is at home.' (But what if no one has said that he *is* at home? What if he is lying upstairs dead?) Too many philosophers maintain, when anxious to explain away negation, that a negation is just a second order affirmation (to the effect that a certain first order affirmation is false), yet, when anxious to explain away falsity, maintain that to assert that a statement is false is just to assert its negation (contradictory). It is impossible to deal with so fundamental a matter here.[22] Let me assert the following merely. Affirmation and negation are exactly on a level, in this sense, that no language can exist which does not contain conventions for both and that both refer to the world equally directly, not to statements about the world: whereas a language can quite well exist without any device to do the work of 'true' and 'false.' Any

---

[22] The following two sets of logical axioms are, as Aristotle (though not his successors) makes them, quite distinct:

(a) No statement can be both true and false.
  No statement can be neither true nor false.
(b) Of two contradictory statements—
  Both cannot be true.
  Both cannot be false.

The second set demands a definition of contradictories, and is usually joined with an unconscious postulate that for every statement there is one and only one other statement such that the pair are contradictories. It is doubtful how far any language does or must contain contradictories, however defined, such as to satisfy both this postulate and the set of axioms (b).

Those of the so-called 'logical paradoxes' (hardly a genuine class) which concern 'true' and 'false' are *not* to be reduced to cases of self-contradiction, any more than 'S but I do not believe it' is. A statement to the effect that it is itself true is every bit as absurd as one to the effect that it is itself false. There are *other* types of sentences which offend against the fundamental conditions of all communication in ways *distinct from* the way in which 'This is red and is not red' offends—e.g., 'This does (I do) not exist,' or equally absurd 'This exists (I exist).' There are more deadly sins than one; nor does the way to salvation lie through any hierarchy.

satisfactory theory of truth must be able to cope equally with falsity:[23] but 'is false' can only be maintained to be logically superfluous by making this fundamental confusion.

5. There is another way of coming to see that the phrase 'is true' is not logically superfluous, and to appreciate what sort of a statement it is to say that a certain statement is true. There are numerous other adjectives which are in the same class as 'true' and 'false,' which are concerned, that is, with the relations between the words (as uttered with reference to an historic situation) and the world, and which nevertheless no one would dismiss as logically superfluous. We say, for example, that a certain statement is exaggerated or vague or bald, a description somewhat rough or misleading or not very good, an account rather general or too concise. In cases like these it is pointless to insist on deciding in simple terms whether the statement is 'true or false.' Is it true or false that Belfast is north of London? That the galaxy is the shape of a fried egg? That Beethoven was a drunkard? That Wellington won the battle of Waterloo? There are various *degrees and dimensions* of success in making statements: the statements fit the facts always more or less loosely, in different ways on different occasions for different intents and purposes. What may score full marks in a general knowledge test may in other circumstances get a gamma. And even the most adroit of languages may fail to 'work' in an abnormal situation or to cope, or cope reasonably simply, with novel discoveries: is it true or false that the dog goes round the cow?[24] What, moreover, of the large class of cases where a statement is not so much false (or true) as out of place, *inept* ('All the signs of bread' said when the bread is before us)?

We become obsessed with 'truth' when discussing statements, just as we become obsessed with 'freedom' when discussing conduct. So long as we think that what has always and alone to be decided is whether a cer-

---

[23] To be false is (not, of course, to correspond to a nonfact, but) to miscorrespond with a fact. Some have not seen how, then, since the statement which is false does not describe the fact with which it miscorresponds (but misdescribes it), we know which fact to compare it with: this was because they thought of all linguistic conventions as descriptive—but it is the demonstrative conventions which fix which situation it is to which the statement refers. No statement can state what it itself refers to.

[24] Here there is much sense in 'coherence' (and pragmatist) theories of truth, despite their failure to appreciate the trite but central point that truth is a matter of the relation between words and world, and despite their wrongheaded *Gleichschaltung* of all varieties of statemental failure under the lone head of 'partly true' (thereafter wrongly equated with 'part of the truth'). 'Correspondence' theorists too often talk as one would who held that every map is either accurate or inaccurate; that accuracy is a single and the sole virtue of a map; that every country can have but one accurate map; that a map on a larger scale or showing different features must be a map of a different country; and so on.

tain action was done freely or was not, we get nowhere: but so soon as we turn instead to the numerous other adverbs used in the same connection ('accidentally,' 'unwillingly,' 'inadvertently,' etc.), things become easier, and we come to see that no concluding inference of the form 'Ergo, it was done freely (or not freely)' is required. Like freedom, truth is a bare minimum or an illusory ideal (the truth, the whole truth and nothing but the truth about, say, the battle of Waterloo or the *Primavera*).[25]

6. Not merely is it jejune to suppose that all a statement aims to be is 'true,' but it may further be questioned whether every 'statement' does aim to be true at all. The principle of Logic, that 'Every proposition must be true or false,' has too long operated as the simplest, most persuasive and most pervasive form of the descriptive fallacy. Philosophers under its influence have forcibly interpreted all 'propositions' on the model of the statement that a certain thing is red, as made when the thing concerned is currently under observation.

Recently, it has come to be realized that many utterances which have been taken to be statements (merely because they are not, on grounds of grammatical form, to be classed as commands, questions, etc.) are not in fact descriptive, nor susceptible of being true or false. When is a statement not a statement? When it is a formula in a calculus: when it is a performatory utterance: when it is a value-judgment: when it is a definition: when it is part of a work of fiction—there are many such suggested answers. It is simply not the business of such utterances to 'correspond to the facts' (and even genuine statements have other businesses besides that of so corresponding).

It is a matter for decision how far we should continue to call such masqueraders 'statements' at all, and how widely we should be prepared to extend the uses of 'true' and 'false' in 'different senses.' My own feeling is that it is better, when once a masquerader has been unmasked, *not* to call it a statement and *not* to say it is true or false. In ordinary life we should not call most of them statements at all, though philosophers and grammarians may have come to do so (or rather, have lumped them all together under the term of art 'proposition'). We make a difference between 'You said you promised' and 'You stated that you promised': the former can mean that you said 'I promise,' whereas the latter must mean that you said 'I promised': the latter, which we say you 'stated,' is something which is true or false, whereas for the former, which is not true or false, we use the wider verb to 'say.' Similarly, there is a difference between 'You say this is (call this) a good picture' and 'You state that this is a good picture.' Moreover, it was only so long as the real nature of arithmetical formulas, say, or of geometrical axioms remained

---

[25] Austin pursues this line of thought further in *How to do things with Words* (Oxford: The Clarendon Press, 1962), pp. 139ff.—(Ed.)

unrecognized, and they were thought to record information about the world, that it was reasonable to call them 'true' (and perhaps even 'statements'—though were they ever so called?) : but, once their nature has been recognized, we no longer feel tempted to call them 'true' or to dispute about their truth or falsity.

In the cases so far considered the model 'This is red' breaks down because the 'statements' assimilated to it are not of a nature to correspond to facts at all—the words are not descriptive words, and so on. But there is also another type of case where the words *are* descriptive words and the 'proposition' does in a way have to correspond to facts, but precisely not in the way that 'This is red' and similar statements setting up to be true have to do.

In the human predicament, for use in which our language is designed, we may wish to speak about states of affairs which have not been observed or are not currently under observation (the future, for example). And although we *can* state anything 'as a fact' (which statement will then be true or false[26]) we need not do so: we need only say 'The cat *may be* on the mat.' This utterance is quite different from tstS—it is not a statement at all (it is not true or false; it is compatible with 'The cat may *not* be on the mat'). In the same way, the situation in which we discuss whether and state that tstS is *true* is different from the situation in which we discuss whether it is *probable* that S. Tst it is probable that S is out of place, inept, in the situation where we can make tstST, and, I think, conversely. It is not our business here to discuss probability: but is worth observing that the phrases 'It is true that' and 'It is probable that' are in the same line of business,[27] and in so far incompatibles.

7. In a recent article in *Analysis,* Mr. Strawson has propounded a view of truth which it will be clear I do not accept. He rejects the 'semantic' account of truth on the perfectly correct ground that the phrase 'is true' is not used in talking about *sentences,* supporting this with an ingenious hypothesis as to how meaning may have come to be confused with truth: but this will not suffice to show what he wants— that 'is true' is not used in talking about (or that 'truth is not a property of') *anything.* For it *is* used in talking about *statements* (which in his article he does not distinguish clearly from sentences). Further, he supports the 'logical superfluity' view to this extent, that he agrees that to say that ST is not to make any further assertion at all, beyond the assertion that S: but he disagrees with it in so far as he thinks that to say that ST *is* to *do* something more than just to assert that S—it is namely

[26] Though it is not yet in place to call it either. For the same reason, one cannot lie or tell the truth about the future.

[27] Compare the odd behaviors of 'was' and 'will be' when attached to 'true' and to 'probable.'

to *confirm* or to *grant* (or something of that kind) the assertion, made or taken as made already, that S. It will be clear that and why I do not accept the first part of this: but what of the second part? I agree that to say that ST 'is' very often, and according to the all-important linguistic occasion, to confirm tstS or to grant it or what not; but this cannot show that to say that ST is not also and at the same time to make an assertion about tstS. To say that I believe you 'is' on occasion to accept your statement; but it is also to make an assertion, which is not made by the strictly performatory utterance 'I accept your statement.' It is common for quite ordinary statements to have a performatory 'aspect': to say that you are a cuckold may be to insult you, but it is also and at the same time to make a statement which is true or false. Mr. Strawson, moreover, seems to confine himself to the case where I *say* 'Your statement is true' or something similar—but what of the case where you state that S and I *say* nothing but *'look and see'* that your statement is true? I do not see how this critical case, to which nothing analogous occurs with strictly performatory utterances, could be made to respond to Mr. Strawson's treatment.

One final point: if it is admitted (*if*) that the rather boring yet satisfactory relation between words and world which has here been discussed does genuinely occur, why should the phrase 'is true' not be our way of describing it? And if it is not, what else is?

TRUTH

P. F. STRAWSON

Mr. Austin offers us a purified version of the correspondence theory of truth. On the one hand he disclaims the semanticists' error of supposing that "true" is a predicate of sentences; on the other, the error of supposing that the relation of correspondence is other than purely conventional, the error which models the word on the world or the world on the word. His own theory is, roughly, that to say that a statement is true is to say that a certain speech-episode is related in a certain conventional way to something in the world exclusive of itself. But neither Mr. Austin's account of the two terms of the truth-conferring relation, nor his account of the relation itself, seems to me satisfactory. The correspondence theory requires, not purification, but elimination.

"Truth," Proceedings of the Aristotelian Society, _Supp. Vol. XXIV_ (1950). _Reprinted by permission of the author and the editor of the Aristotelian Society._

1. STATEMENTS

It is, of course, indisputable that we use various substantival expressions as grammatical subjects of "true." These are, commonly, noun-phrases like "What he said" or "His statement"; or pronouns or noun-phrases, with a "that"-clause in apposition, e.g., "It . . . that p" and "The statement that p." Austin proposes that we should use "statement" to do general duty for such expressions as these. I have no objection. This will enable us to say, in a philosophically noncommittal way, that, in using "true," we are talking about statements. By "saying this in a non-committal way," I mean saying it in a way which does not commit us to any view about the nature of statements so talked about; which does not commit us, for example, to the view that statements so talked about are historic events.

The words "assertion" and "statement" have a parallel and convenient duplicity of sense. "My statement" may be either what I say or my saying it. My saying something is certainly an episode. What I say is not. It is the latter, not the former, we declare to be true. (Speaking the truth is not a manner of speaking: it is saying something true.) When we say "His statement was received with thunderous applause" or "His vehement assertion was followed by a startled silence," we are certainly referring to, characterizing, a historic event, and placing it in the context of others. If I say that the same statement was first whispered by John and then bellowed by Peter, uttered first in French and repeated in English, I am plainly still making historical remarks about utterance-occasions; but the word "statement" has detached itself from reference to any particular speech-episode. The episodes I am talking about are the whisperings, bellowings, utterings, and repetitions. The statement is not something that figures in all these episodes. Nor, when I say that the statement is true, as opposed to saying that it was, in these various ways, made, am I talking indirectly about these episodes or any episodes at all. (Saying of a statement that it is true is not related to saying of a speech-episode that it was true as saying of a statement that it was whispered is related to saying of a speech-episode that it was a whisper.) It is futile to ask what thing or event I *am* talking about (over and above the subject-matter of the statement) in declaring a statement to be true; for there is no such thing or event. The word "statement" and the phrase "What he said," like the conjunction "that" followed by a noun clause, are convenient, grammatically substantival, devices, which we employ, on certain occasions, for certain purposes, notably (but not only) the occasions on which we use the word "true." What these occasions are I shall try later to elucidate. To suppose that, whenever we use a singular sub-stantive, we are, or ought to be, using it to refer to something, is an ancient, but no longer a respectable, error.

More plausible than the thesis that in declaring a statement to be true I am talking about a speech-episode is the thesis that in order for me to declare a statement true, there must have occurred, within my knowledge, at least one episode which was a making of that statement. This is largely, but (as Austin sees) not entirely, correct. The occasion of my declaring a statement to be true may be not that someone has made the statement, but that I am envisaging the possibility of someone's making it. For instance, in discussing the merits of the Welfare State, I might say: "It is true that the general health of the community has improved (that p), but this is due only to the advance in medical science." It is not necessary that anyone should have said that p, in order for this to be a perfectly proper observation. In making it, I am not talking *about* an actual or possible speech-episode. I am myself asserting that p, in a certain way, with a certain purpose. I am anticipatorily conceding, in order to neutralize, a possible objection. I forestall someone's making the state-ment that p by making it myself, with additions. It is of prime importance to distinguish the fact that the use of "true" always glances backwards or forwards to the actual or envisaged making of a statement by someone, from the theory that it is used to characterize such (actual or possible) episodes.

It is not easy to explain the nonepisodic and noncommittal sense of "statement" in which "statement" = "what is said to be true or false." But, at the risk of being tedious, I shall pursue the subject. For if Austin is right in the suggestion that it is basically of speech-episodes that we predicate "true," it should be possible to "reduce" assertions in which we say of a statement in the nonepisodic sense that it is true to assertions in which we are predicating truth of episodes. Austin points out that the same sentence may be used to make different statements. He would no doubt agree that different sentences may be used to make the same state-ment. I am not thinking only of different languages or synonymous ex-pressions in the same language; but also of such occasions as that on which you say of Jones "He is ill," I say *to* Jones "You are ill," and Jones says "I am ill." Using, not only different sentences, but sentences with different meanings, we all make "the same statement"; and this is the sense of "statement" we need to discuss, since it is, *prima facie,* of state-ments in this sense that we say that they are true or false (e.g., "What they all said, namely, that Jones was ill, was quite true.") We could say: People make the same statement when the words they use in the situations in which they use them are such that they must (logically) either all be making a true statement or all be making a false statement. But this is to use "true" in the elucidation of "same statement." Or we could say, of the present case: Jones, you, and I all make the same statement because, using the words we used in the situation in which we used them, we were all applying the same description to the same person at a certain moment in his history; anyone applying that description to that person (etc.), would be making that statement. Mr. Austin might then wish to analyze (A) "The statement that Jones was ill is true" in some such way as the following: "If anyone has uttered, or were to utter, words such that in the situation in which they are uttered, he is applying to a person the same description as I apply to that person when I now utter the words 'Jones was ill,' then the resulting speech-episode was, or would be, true." It seems plain, however, that nothing but the desire to find a metaphysically irreproachable first term for the correspondence relation could induce anyone to accept this analysis of (A) as an elaborate general hypothetical. It would be a plausible suggestion only if the grammatical subjects of "true" were *commonly* expressions referring to particular, uniquely dateable, speech-episodes. But the simple and obvious fact is that the expressions occurring as such grammatical subjects ("What they said," "It . . . that *p*," and so on) never do, in these contexts, stand for such episodes.[1] *What they said* has no date, though their several sayings of it are dateable. *The statement that p* is not an event, though it had to be made for the first time and made within my knowledge if I am to talk of its truth or falsity. If I endorse Plato's view, wrongly attributing it to Lord Russell ("Russell's view that *p* is quite true"), and am corrected, I have not discovered that I was talking of an event separated by centuries from the one I imagined I was talking of. (Corrected, I may say: "Well it's true, whoever said it.") My *implied* historical judgment is false; that is all.

2. FACTS

What of the second term of the correspondence relation? For this Mr. Austin uses the following words or phrases: "thing," "event," "situation," "state of affairs," "feature," and "fact." All these are words which should be handled with care. I think that through failing to discriminate sufficiently between them, Mr. Austin (1) encourages the assimilation of facts to things, or (what is approximately the same

---

[1] And the cases where such phrases might most plausibly be exhibited as having an episode-referring role are precisely those which yield most readily to another treatment; viz., those in which one speaker corroborates, confirms, or grants what another has just said (see Sec. 4 below).

thing) of stating to referring; (2) misrepresents the use of "true"; and (3) obscures another and more fundamental problem.

In Section 3 of his paper, Mr. Austin says, or suggests, that all stating involves both referring ("demonstration") and characterizing ("description"). It is questionable whether all statements do involve both,[2] though it is certain that some do. The following sentences, for example, could all be used to make such statements; i.e., statements in the making of which both the referring and describing functions are performed, the performance of the two functions being approximately (though not exclusively) assignable to different parts of the sentences as uttered:

> The cat has the mange.
> That parrot talks a lot.
> Her escort was a man of medium build, clean-shaven, well-dressed and with a North Country accent.

In using such sentences to make statements, we refer to a thing or person (object) in order to go on to characterize it (we demonstrate in order to describe). *A reference* can be correct or incorrect. A *description* can fit, or fail to fit, the thing or person to which it is applied.[3] When we refer correctly, there certainly is a conventionally established relation between the words, so used, and the thing to which we refer. When we describe correctly, there certainly is a conventionally established relation between the words we use in describing and the type of thing or person we describe. These relations, as Mr. Austin emphasizes, are different. An expression used referringly has a different logical role from an expression used describingly. They are differently related to the object. And *stating* is different from referring, and different from describing; for it is (in such cases) both these at once. Statement (*some* statement) is reference-cum-description. To avoid cumbersome phrasing, I shall speak henceforward of *parts* of statements (the referring part and the describing part); though parts of statements are no more to be equated with parts of sentences (or parts of speech-episodes) than statements are to be equated with sentences (or speech-episodes).

That (person, thing, etc.) to which the referring part of the statement refers, and which the describing part of the statement fits or fails to fit, is that which the statement is *about*. It is evident that there is nothing else in the world for the statement itself to be related to either

---

[2] See Sec. 5 below. The thesis that all statements involve both demonstration and description is, roughly, the thesis that all statements are, or involve. subject-predicate statements (not excluding relational statements).

[3] Cf. the phrase "He is described as . . . ." What fills the gap is not a sentence (expression which could normally be used to make a statement), but a phrase which could occur as a part of an expression so used.

in some further way of its own or in either of the different ways in which these different parts of the statement are related to what the statement is about. And it is evident that the demand that there should be such a relatum is logically absurd: a logically fundamental type-mistake. But the demand for something in the world *which makes the statement true* (Mr. Austin's phrase), or *to which the statement corresponds when it is true,* is just this demand. And the answering theory that to say that a statement is true is to say that a speech-episode is conventionally related in a certain way to such a relatum reproduces the type-error embodied in this demand. For while we certainly say that a statement corresponds to (fits, is borne out by, agrees with) the facts, as a variant on saying that it is true, we *never* say that a statement corresponds to the thing, person, etc., it is about. What "makes the statement" that the cat has mange "true," is not the cat, but the *condition* of the cat, i.e., the fact that the cat has mange. The only plausible candidate for the position of what (in the world) makes the statement true is the fact it states; but the fact it states is not something in the world.[4] It is not an object; not even (as some have supposed) a complex object consisting of one or more particular elements (constituents, parts) and a universal element (constituent, part). I can (perhaps) hand you, or draw a circle round, or time with a stop-watch the things or incidents that are referred to when a statement is made. Statements are about such objects; but they state facts. Mr. Austin seems to ignore the complete difference of type between, e.g., "fact" and "thing"; to talk as if "fact" were just a very general word (with, unfortunately, some misleading features) for "event," "thing," etc., instead of being (as it is) both wholly different from these, and yet the only possible candidate for the desired nonlinguistic correlate of "statement." Roughly: The thing, person, etc., referred to is the material correlate of the referring part of the statement; the quality or property the referent is said to "possess" is the *pseudo*material correlate of its describing part; and the fact to which the statement "corresponds" is the *pseudo*material correlate of the statement as a whole.

These points are, of course, reflected in the behavior of the word "fact" in ordinary language; behavior which Mr. Austin notes, but by which he is insufficiently warned. "Fact," like "true," "states," and

---

[4] This is not, of course, to deny that there is that in the world which a statement of this kind is about (true or false *of*), which is *referred to* and *described* and which the description fits (if the statement is true) or fails to fit (if it is false). This truism is an inadequate introduction to the task of elucidating, not our use of "true," but a certain general way of using language, a certain type of discourse, viz., the fact-stating type of discourse. What confuses the issue about the use of the word "true" is precisely its entanglement with this much more fundamental and difficult problem. [See (ii) of this section.]

"statement" is wedded to "that"-clauses; and there is nothing unholy about this union. Facts are known, stated, learned, forgotten, overlooked, commented on, communicated, or noticed. (Each of these verbs may be followed by a "that"-clause or a "the fact that"-clause.) Facts are what statements (when true) state; they are not what statements are about. They are not, like things or happenings on the face of the globe, witnessed or heard or seen, broken or overturned, interrupted or prolonged, kicked, destroyed, mended or noisy. Mr. Austin notes the expression "fact that," warns us that it may tempt us to identify facts with true statements and explains its existence by saying that for certain purposes in ordinary life we neglect, or take as irrelevant, the distinction between saying something true and the thing or episode of which we are talking. It would indeed be wrong—but not for Mr. Austin's reasons—to identify "fact" and "true statement"; for these expressions have different roles in our language, as can be seen by the experiment of trying to interchange them in context. Nevertheless, their roles—or those of related expressions—overlap. There is no nuance, except of style, between "That's true" and "That's a fact"; nor between "Is it true that . . . ?" and "Is it a fact that . . . ?" [5] But Mr. Austin's reasons for objecting to the identification seem mistaken, as does his explanation of the usage which (he says) tempts us to make it. Because he thinks of a statement as something in the world (a speech-episode) and a fact as something else in the world (what the statement either "corresponds to" or "is about"), he conceives the distinction as of overriding importance in philosophy, though (surprisingly) sometimes negligible for ordinary purposes. But I can conceive of no occasion on which I could possibly be held to be "neglecting or taking as irrelevant" the distinction between, say, my wife's bearing me twins (at midnight) and my saying (ten minutes later) that my wife had borne me twins. On Mr. Austin's thesis, however, my announcing "The fact is that my wife has borne me twins" would be just such an occasion.

Elsewhere in his paper, Mr. Austin expresses the fact that there is no theoretical limit to what could truly be said about things in the world, while there are very definite practical limits to what human beings actually can and do say about them, by the remark that statements "always fit the facts more or less loosely, in different ways for different purposes." But what could fit more perfectly the fact that it is raining than the

---

[5] I think in general the difference between them is that while the use of "true," as already acknowledged, glances backwards or forwards at an actual or envisaged making of a statement, the use of "fact" does not generally do this though it may do it sometimes. It certainly does not do it in, e.g., the phrase "The fact is that . . ." which serves rather to prepare us for the unexpected and unwelcome.

statement that it is raining? Of course, statements and facts fit. They were made for each other. If you prize the statements off the world you prize the facts off it too; but the world would be none the poorer. (You don't also prize off the world what the statements are about—for this you would need a different kind of lever.)

A symptom of Mr. Austin's uneasiness about facts is his preference for the expressions "situation" and "state of affairs"; expressions of which the character and function are a little less transparent than those of "fact." They are more plausible candidates for inclusion in the world. For while it is true that situations and states of affairs are not seen or heard (any more than facts are), but are rather *summed up* or *taken in at a glance* (phrases which stress the connection with statement and "that"-clause respectively), it is also true that there is a sense of "about" in which we do talk about, do describe, situations and states of affairs. We say, for example, "The international situation is serious" or "This state of affairs lasted from the death of the King till the dissolution of Parliament." In the same sense of "about," we talk about facts; as when we say "I am alarmed by the fact that kitchen expenditure has risen by 50 per cent in the last year." But whereas "fact" in such usages is linked with a "that"-clause (or connected no less obviously with "statement," as when we "take down the facts" or hand someone the facts on a sheet of paper), "situation" and "state of affairs" stand by themselves, states of affairs are said to have a beginning and an end, and so on. Nevertheless, situations and states of affairs so talked of are (like facts so talked of), abstractions that a logician, if not a grammarian, should be able to see through. Being alarmed by a fact is not like being frightened by a shadow. It is being alarmed because. . . . One of the most economical and pervasive devices of language is the use of substantival expressions to abbreviate, summarize, and connect. Having made a series of descriptive statements, I can comprehensively connect with these the remainder of my discourse by the use of such expressions as "this situation" or "this state of affairs"; just as, having produced what I regard as a set of reasons for a certain conclusion I allow myself to draw breath by saying "Since *these things* are so, then . . . ," instead of prefacing the entire story by the conjunction. A situation or state of affairs is, roughly, a set of facts, not a set of things.

A point which it is important to notice in view of Mr. Austin's use of these expressions (in Sections 3a and 3b of his paper) is that when we *do* "talk about" situations (as opposed to things and persons) the situation we talk about is not, as he seems to think it is, correctly identified with the fact we state (with "what makes the statement true"). If a situation is the "subject" of our statement, then what "makes the statement true" is not the situation, but the fact that the situation has the character it is asserted to have. I think much of the persuasiveness of the phrase "talking about situations" derives from that use of the word on which I have just commented. But if a situation is treated as the "subject" of a statement, then it will not serve as the nonlinguistic term, for which Mr. Austin is seeking, of the "relation of correspondence"; and if it is treated as the nonlinguistic term of this relation, it will not serve as the subject of the statement.

Someone might now say: "No doubt 'situation,' 'state of affairs,' 'facts' are related in this way to 'that'-clauses and assertive sentences; can serve, in certain ways and for certain purposes, as indefinite stand-ins for specific expressions of these various types. So also is 'thing' related to some nouns; 'event' to some verbs, nouns, and sentences; 'quality' to some adjectives; 'relation' to some nouns, verbs, and adjectives. Why manifest this prejudice in favor of things and events as alone being parts of the world or its history? Why not situations and facts as well?" The answer to this (implicit in what has gone before) is twofold.

(i) The first part of the answer[6] is that the whole charm of talking of situations, states of affairs, or facts as included in, or parts of, the world, consists in thinking of them as things, and groups of things; that the temptation to talk of situations, etc., in the idiom appropriate to talking of things and events is, once this first step is taken, overwhelming. Mr. Austin does not withstand it. He significantly slips in the word "feature" (noses and hills are *features,* of faces and landscapes) as a substitute for "facts." He says that the reason why photographs and maps are not "true" in the way that statements are true is that the relation of a map or a photograph to what it is a map or a photograph of is not wholly (in the first case) and not at all (in the second) a conventional relation. But this is not the only, or the fundamental, reason. (The relation between the Prime Minister of England and the phrase "the Prime Minister of England" *is* conventional; but it doesn't make sense to say that someone uttering the phrase out of context is saying something true or false.) The (for present purposes) fundamental reason is that "being a map of" or "being a photograph of" *are* relations, of which the non-photographic, noncartographical, relata are, say, personal or geographical *entities.* The trouble with correspondence theories of truth is not primarily the tendency to substitute nonconventional relations for what is really a wholly conventional relation. It is the misrepresentation of "correspondence between statement and fact" *as a relation, of any kind, between events or things or groups of things* that is the trouble. Cor-

---

[6] Which could be more shortly expressed by saying that if we read "world" (a sadly corrupted word) as "heavens and earth," talk of facts, situations, and states of affairs, as "included in" or "parts of" the world is, obviously, metaphorical. The world is the totality of things, not of facts.

respondence theorists think of a statement as "describing that which makes it true" (fact, situation, state of affairs) in the way a descriptive predicate may be used to describe, or a referring expression to refer to, a thing.[7]

(ii) The second objection to Mr. Austin's treatment of facts, situations, states of affairs as "parts of the world" which we declare to stand in a certain relation to a statement when we declare that statement true, goes deeper than the preceding one but is, in a sense, its point. Mr. Austin rightly says or implies (Section 3) that for some of the purposes for which we use language, there must be conventions correlating the words of our language with what is to be found in the world. Not all the linguistic purposes for which this necessity holds, however, are identical. Orders, as well as information, are conventionally communicated. Suppose "orange" always meant what we mean by "Bring me an orange" and "that orange" always meant what we mean by "Bring me that orange," and, in general, our language contained only sentences in some such way imperative. There would be no less need for a conventional correlation between the word and the world. Nor would there be any less to be found in the world. But those pseudoentities which *make statements true* would not figure among the nonlinguistic correlates. They would no more be found; (they never were found, and never did figure among the nonlinguistic correlates). The point is that the word "fact" (and the "set-of-facts" words like "situation" and "state of affairs") have, like the words "statement" and "true" themselves, a certain type of word-world-relating discourse (the informative) *built in* to them. The occurrence in ordinary discourse of the words "fact," "statement," "true" signalizes the occurrence of this type of discourse; just as the occurrence

---

[7] Suppose the pieces set on a chessboard, a game in progress. And suppose someone gives, in words, an exhaustive statement of the position of the pieces. Mr. Austin's objection (or one of his objections) to earlier correspondence theories is that they would represent the relation between the description and the board with the pieces on it as like, say, the relation between a newspaper diagram of a chess problem and a board with the pieces correspondingly arranged. He says, rather, that the relation is a purely conventional one. My objection goes farther. It is that there is no thing or event called "a statement" (though there is the making of the statement) and there is no thing or event called "a fact" or "situation" (though there is the chessboard with the pieces on it) which stand to one another in any, even a purely conventional, relation as the newspaper diagram stands to the board-and-pieces. The facts (situation, state of affairs) cannot, like the chessboard-and-pieces, have coffee spilled on them or be upset by a careless hand. It is because Mr. Austin needs such events and things for his theory that he takes the making of the statement as the statement, and that which the statement is about as the fact which it states.

Events can be dated and things can be located. But the facts which statements (when true) state can be neither dated nor located. (Nor can the statements, though the making of them can be.) Are they included in the world?

of the words "order," "obeyed" signalizes the occurrence of another kind of conventional communication (the imperative). If our task were to elucidate the nature of the first type of discourse, it would be futile to attempt to do it in terms of the words "fact," "statement," "true," for these words contain the problem, not its solution. It would, for the same reason, be equally futile to attempt to elucidate any one of these words (in so far as the elucidation of *that* word would be the elucidation of *this* problem) in terms of the others. And it is, indeed, very strange that people have so often proceeded by saying "Well, we're pretty clear what a statement is, aren't we? Now let us settle *the further question,* viz., what it is for a statement to be true." This is like "Well, we're clear about what a command is: now what is it for a command to be obeyed?" As if one could divorce statements and commands from the point of making or giving them!

Suppose we had in our language the word "execution" meaning "action which is the carrying out of a command." And suppose someone asked the philosophical question: What is *obedience?* What is it for a command to be *obeyed?* A philosopher might produce the answer: "Obedience is a conventional relation between a command and an execution. A command is obeyed when it corresponds to an execution."

This is the Correspondence Theory of Obedience. It has, perhaps, a little less value as an attempt to elucidate the nature of one type of communication than the Correspondence Theory of Truth has as an attempt to elucidate that of another. In both cases, the words occurring in the solution incorporate the problem. And, of course, this intimate relation between "statement" and "fact" (which is understood when it is seen that they both incorporate this problem) explains why it is that when we seek to explain *truth* on the model of naming or classifying or any other kind of conventional or nonconventional relation between one thing and another, we always find ourselves landed with "fact," "situation," "state of affairs" as the nonlinguistic terms of the relation.

But why should the problem of Truth (the problem about our use of "true") be seen as this problem of elucidating the fact-stating type of discourse? The answer is that it shouldn't be; but that the Correspondence Theory can only be fully seen through when it is seen as a barren attempt on this second problem. Of course, a philosopher concerned with the second problem, concerned to elucidate a certain general type of discourse, must stand back from language and talk about the different ways in which utterances are related to the world (though he must get beyond "correspondence of statement and fact" if his talk is to be fruitful). But— to recur to something I said earlier—the occurrence *in ordinary discourse* of the words "true," "fact," etc., signalizes, without commenting on, the occurrence of a certain way of using language. When we use these words in ordinary life, we are talking within, and not about, a certain frame of discourse; we are precisely not talking about the way in which utterances are, or may be, conventionally related to the world. We are talking about persons and things, but in a way in which we could not talk about them if conditions of certain kinds were not fulfilled. The problem about the use of "true" is to see how this word fits into that frame of discourse. The surest route to the wrong answer is to confuse this problem with the question: What type of discourse is this?[8]

3. CONVENTIONAL CORRESPONDENCE

It will be clear from the previous paragraph what I think wrong with Mr. Austin's account of the relation itself, as opposed to its terms. In Section 4 of his paper he says that, when we declare a statement to be true, the relation between the statement and the world which our declaration "asserts to obtain" is "a purely conventional relation" and "one which we could alter at will." This remark reveals the fundamental confusion of which Mr. Austin is guilty between:

(*a*) the semantic conditions which must be satisfied for the statement that a certain statement is true to be itself true; and

(*b*) what is asserted when a certain statement is stated to be true.

Suppose A makes a statement, and B declares A's statement to be true. Then for B's statement to be true, it is, *of course,* necessary that the words used by A in making the statement should stand in a certain conventional (semantical) relationship with the world; and that the "linguistic rules" underlying this relationship should be rules "observed" by both A and B. It should be remarked that these conditions (with the exception of the condition about B's observance of linguistic rules) are equally necessary conditions of A's having made a true statement in using the words he used. *It is no more and no less absurd to suggest that B, in making his statement, asserts that these semantic conditions are fulfilled than it is to suggest that A, in making his statement, asserts that these semantic conditions are fulfilled* (i.e., that we can never use words without mentioning them). *If* Mr. Austin is right in suggesting that to say that a statement is true is to say that "the historic state of affairs to which it (i.e., for Mr. Austin, the episode of making it) is correlated by the demonstrative conventions (the one it 'refers to') is of a type with which the sentence used in making the statement is correlated by

---

[8] A parallel mistake would be to think that in our ordinary use (as opposed to a philosopher's use) of the word "quality," we were talking about people's uses of words; on the ground (correct in itself) that this word would have no use but for the occurrence of a certain general way of using words.

the descriptive conventions," *then* (and this is shown quite clearly by his saying that the relation we assert to obtain is a "purely conventional one" which "could be altered at will") in declaring a statement to be true, we are either:

> (*a*) talking about the meanings of the words used by the speaker whose making of the statement is the occasion for our use of "true" (i.e., profiting by the occasion to give semantic rules) ; or
> (*b*) saying that the speaker has used correctly the words he did use.

It is *patently* false that we are doing either of these things. Certainly, we use the word "true" when the semantic conditions described by Austin[9] are fulfilled; but we do not, in using the word, *state* that they are fulfilled. (And this, incidentally, is the answer to the question with which Mr. Austin concludes his paper.) The damage is done (the two problems distinguished at the end of the previous section confused) by asking the question: *When* do we use the word "true"? instead of the question: *How* do we use the word "true"?

Someone says: "It's true that French Governments rarely last more than a few months, but the electoral system is responsible for that." Is the fact he states in the first part of his sentence alterable by changing the conventions of language? It is not.

4. USES OF "THAT"-CLAUSES; AND OF "STATEMENT," "TRUE," "FACT," "EXAGGERATED," ETC.

(*a*) There are many ways of making an assertion about a thing, X, besides the bare use of the sentence-pattern "X is Y." Many of these involve the use of "that"-clauses. For example:

---

[9] In what, owing to his use of the words "statement," "fact," "situation," etc., is a misleading form. The quoted account of the conditions of truthful statement is more nearly appropriate as an account of the conditions of correct descriptive reference. Suppose, in a room with a bird in a cage, I say "That parrot is very talkative." Then my use of the referring expression ("That parrot") with which my sentence begins is correct when the token-object (bird) with which my token-expression (event) is correlated by the conventions of demonstration is of a kind with which the type-expression is correlated by the conventions of description. Here we do have an event and a thing and a (type-mediated) conventional relation between them. If someone corrects me, saying "That's not a parrot; it's a cockatoo," he may be correcting either a linguistic or a factual error on my part. (The question of which he is doing is the question of whether I would have stuck to my story on a closer examination of the bird.) Only in the former case is he declaring a certain semantic condition to be unfulfilled. In the latter case, he is talking about the bird. He asserts that it is a cockatoo and not a parrot. This he could have done whether I had spoken or not. He also *corrects* me, which he could not have done if I had not spoken.

How often shall I have to tell you ⎫
Today I learned   ⎪
It is surprising   ⎪
The fact is
I have just been reminded of the fact ⎬ that X is Y.
It is indisputable   ⎪
It is true   ⎪
It is established beyond question   ⎭

These are all ways of asserting, in very different context and circumstances, that X is Y.[10] Some of them involve autobiographical assertions as well; others do not. In the grammatical sense already conceded, all of them are "about" facts or statements. In no other sense is any of them about either, though some of them carry *implications* about the *making* of statements.

(*b*) There are many different circumstances in which the simple sentence-pattern "X is Y" may be used to do things which are not merely stating (though they all involve stating) that X is Y. In uttering words of this simple pattern we may be encouraging, reproving, or warning someone; reminding someone; answering, or replying to, someone; denying what someone has said; confirming, granting, corroborating, agreeing with, admitting what someone has said. Which of these, if any, we are doing depends on the circumstances in which, using this simple sentence-pattern, we assert that X is Y.

(*c*) In many of the cases in which we are doing something besides merely stating that X is Y, we have available, for use in suitable contexts, certain abbreviatory devices which enable us to state that X is Y (to make our denial, answer, admission, or whatnot) *without* using the sentence-pattern "X is Y." Thus, if someone asks us "Is X Y?," we may state (in the way of reply) that X is Y by saying "Yes." If someone says "X is Y," we may state (in the way of denial) that X is not Y, by saying "It is not" or by saying "That's not true"; or we may state (in the way of corroboration, agreement, granting, etc.) that X is Y by saying "It is indeed" or "That is true." In all these cases (of reply, denial, and agreement) the context of our utterance, as well as the words we use, must be taken into account if it is to be clear what we are asserting, viz., that X is (or is not) Y. It seems to me plain that in these cases "true" and "not true" (we rarely use "false") are functioning as abbreviatory statement-devices of the same general kind as the others quoted. And it seems also plain that the *only* difference between these

---

[10] One might prefer to say that in some of these cases one was asserting only *by implication* that X is Y; though it seems to me more probable that in all these cases we should say, of the speaker, not "What he said implied that X is Y," but "He *said* that X was Y."

devices which might tempt us, while saying of some ("Yes," "It is indeed," "It is not") that, in using them, we were talking about X, to say of others ("That's true," "That's not true") that, in using them, we were talking about something quite different, viz., the utterance which was the occasion for our use of these devices, is their difference in grammatical structure, i.e., the fact that "true" occurs as a grammatical predicate.[11] (It is obviously not a predicate of X.) If Mr. Austin's thesis, that in using the word "true" we make an assertion about a statement, were no more than the thesis that the word "true" occurs as a grammatical predicate, with, as grammatical subjects, such words and phrases as "That," "What he said," "His statement," etc., then, of course, it would be indisputable. It is plain, however, that he means more than this, and I have already produced my objections to the more that he means.

(d) It will be clear that, in common with Mr. Austin, I reject the thesis that the phrase "is true" is logically superfluous, together with the thesis that to say that a proposition is true is *just* to assert it and to say that it is false is *just* to assert its contradictory. "True" and "not true" have jobs of their own to do, *some,* but by no means all, of which I have characterized above. In using them, we are not *just* asserting that X is Y or that X is not Y. We are asserting this in a way in which we could not assert it unless certain conditions were fulfilled; we may also be granting, denying, confirming, etc. It will be clear also that the rejection of these two theses does not entail acceptance of Mr. Austin's thesis that in using "true" we are making an assertion about a statement. Nor does it entail the rejection of the thesis which Mr. Austin (in Section 4 of his paper) couples with these two, viz., the thesis that to say that an assertion is true is not to make any further *assertion* at all. This thesis holds for many uses, but requires modification for others.

(e) The occasions for using "true" mentioned so far in this section are evidently not the only occasions of its use. There is, for example, the generally concessive employment of "It is true that *p* . . . ," which it is difficult to see how Mr. Austin could accommodate. All these occasions have, however, a certain contextual immediacy which is obviously absent when we utter such sentences as "What John said yesterday is quite true" and "What La Rochefoucauld said about friendship is true." Here the context of our utterance does not identify for us the statement we are

---

[11] Compare also the English habit of making a statement followed by an interrogative appeal for agreement in such forms as "isn't it?," "doesn't he?," etc., with the corresponding German and Italian idioms, "Nicht wahr?," "non è vero?" There is surely no significant difference between the phrases which do not employ the word for "true" and those which do: they all appeal for agreement in the same way.

talking about (in the philosophically noncommittal sense in which we *are* "talking about statements" when we use the word "true"), and so we use a descriptive phrase to do the job. But the descriptive phrase does not identify an event; though the statement we make carries the implication (in some sense of "implication") that there occurred an event which was John's making yesterday (or Rochefoucauld's making sometime) the statement that p (i.e., the statement we declare to be true). We are certainly not telling our audience that the event occurred, e.g., that John made the statement that p, for (i) we do not state, either by way of quotation or otherwise, what it was that John said yesterday, and (ii) our utterance achieves its main purpose (that of making, by way of confirmation or endorsement, the statement that p) only if our audience already knows that John yesterday made the statement that p. The abbreviatory function of "true" in cases such as these becomes clearer if we compare them with what we say in the case where (i) we want to assert that p; (ii) we want to indicate (or display our knowledge that) an event occurred which was John's making yesterday the statement that p; (iii) we believe our audience ignorant or forgetful of the fact that John said yesterday that p. We then use the formula "As John said yesterday, p" or "It is true, as John said yesterday, that p," or "What John said yesterday, namely that p, is true." (Of course the words represented by the letter p, which we use, may be—sometimes, if we are to make the same statement, must be—different from the words which John used.) Sometimes, to embarrass, or test, our audience, we use, in cases where the third of these conditions is fulfilled, the formula appropriate to its nonfulfilment, viz., "What John said yesterday is true."

(*f*) In criticism of my view of truth put forward in *Analysis*,[12] and presumably in support of his own thesis that "true" is used to assert that a certain relation obtains between a speech-episode and something in the world exclusive of that episode, Mr. Austin makes, in Section 7 of his paper, the following point. He says: "Mr. Strawson seems to confine himself to the case when I say "Your statement is true" or something similar—but what of the case when you state that S and I say nothing, but *look and see* that your statement is true?" The point of the objection is, I suppose, that since I *say* nothing, I cannot be making any performatory use of "true"; yet I can see *that* your statement is true. The example, however, seems to have a force precisely contrary to what Mr. Austin intended. Of course, "true" has a different role in "X sees that Y's statement is true" from its role in "Y's statement is true." What is this role? Austin says in my hearing "There is a cat on the mat" and I look and see a cat on the mat. Someone (Z) reports: "Strawson saw that Austin's statement was true." What is he reporting?

[12] Vol. IX, No. 6 (1949).

He is reporting that I have seen a cat on the mat; but he is reporting this in a way in which he could not report it except in certain circumstances, viz., in the circumstances of Austin's having said in my hearing that there was a cat on the mat. Z's remark also carries the implication that Austin made a statement, but cannot be regarded as *reporting* this by implication since it fulfils its main purpose only if the audience already knows that Austin made a statement and what statement he made; and the implication (which *can* be regarded as an implied report) that I heard and understood what Austin said.[13] The man who looks and sees that the statement that there is a cat on the mat is true, sees no more and no less than the man who looks and sees that there is a cat on the mat, or the man who looks and sees that there is *indeed* a cat on the mat. But the *settings* of the first and third cases may be different from that of the second.

This example has value, however. It emphasizes the importance of the concept of the "occasion" on which we may make use of the assertive device which is the subject of this symposium (the word "true"); and minimizes (what I was inclined to overemphasize) the performatory character of our uses of it.

(*g*) Mr. Austin stresses the differences between negation and falsity; rightly, in so far as to do so is to stress the difference (of occasion and context) between asserting that X is not Y and denying the assertion that X is Y. He also exaggerates the difference; for, if I have taken the point of his example, he suggests that there are cases in which "X is not Y" is inappropriate to a situation in which, if anyone stated that X was Y, it would be correct to say that the statement that X was Y was false. These are cases where the question of whether X is or is not Y does not arise (where the conditions of its arising are not fulfilled). They are equally, it seems to me, cases when the question of the truth or falsity of the statement that X is Y does not arise.

(*h*) A qualification of my general thesis, that in using "true" and "untrue" we are not talking about a speech-episode, is required to allow for those cases where our interest is not primarily in what the speaker asserts, but in the speaker's asserting it, in, say, the fact of his having *told the truth* rather than in the fact which he reported in doing so. (We may, of course, be interested in both; or our interest in a man's evident truthfulness on one occasion may be due to our concern with the degree of his reliability on others.)

But this case calls for no special analysis and presents no handle to any theorist of truth; for to use "true" in this way is simply to charac-

---

[13] If *I* report: "I see that Austin's statement is true," this is simply a first-hand corroborative report that there is a cat on the mat, made in a way in which it could not be made except in these circumstances.

terize a certain *event* as *the making,* by someone, of a true statement. The problem of analysis remains.

(*i*) Mr. Austin says that we shall find it easier to be clear about "true" if we consider other adjectives "in the same class," such as "exaggerated," "vague," "rough," "misleading," "general," "too concise." I do not think these words *are* in quite the same class as "true" and "false." In any language in which statements can be made at all, it must be possible to make true and false statements. But statements can suffer from the further defects Mr. Austin mentions only when language has attained a certain richness. Imagine one of Mr. Austin's rudimentary languages with "single words" for "complex situations" of totally different kinds. One could make true or false statements; but not statements which were exaggerated, overconcise, too general, or rather rough. And even given a language as rich as you please, whereas all statements made in it could be true or false, not all statements could be exaggerated. When can we say that the statement that p is exaggerated? *One* of the conditions is this: that, if the sentence S_1 is used to make the statement that p, there should be some sentence S_2 (which could be used to make the statement that q) such that S_1 and S_2 are related somewhat as "There were 200 people there" is related to "There were 100 people there." (To the remark "We got married yesterday," you cannot, except as a joke, reply: "You are exaggerating.")

Mr. Austin's belief, then, that the word "exaggerated" stands for a relation between a statement and something in the world exclusive of the statement, would at least be an oversimplification, even if it were not objectionable in other ways. But it is objectionable in other ways. The difficulties about statement and fact recur; and the difficulties about the relation. Mr. Austin would not want to say that the relation between an exaggerated statement and the world was like that between a glove and a hand too small for it. He would say that the relation was a conventional one. But the fact that the statement that p is exaggerated is not in any sense a conventional fact. (It is, perhaps, the fact that there were 1,200 people there and not 2,000.) If a man says: "There were at least 2,000 people there," you may reply (A) "No, there were not so many (far more)," or you may reply (B) "That's an exaggeration (understatement)." (A) and (B) say the same thing. Look at the situation more closely. In saying (A), you are not merely asserting that there were fewer than 2,000 people there: you are also correcting the first speaker, and correcting him in a certain general way, which you could not have done if he had not spoken as he did, though you could merely have asserted that there were fewer than 2,000 there without his having spoken. Notice also that what is being asserted by the use of (A)— that there were fewer than 2,000 there—cannot be understood without

taking into account the original remark which was the occasion for
(A). (A) has both contextually assertive and performatory features.
(B) has the same features, and does the same job as (A), but more
concisely and with greater contextual reliance.

Not all the words taken by Austin as likely to help us to be clear
about "true" are in the same class as one another. "Exaggerated" is, of
those he mentions, the one most relevant to his thesis; but has been seen
to yield to my treatment. Being "overconcise" and "too general" are
not ways of being "not quite true." These obviously relate to the specific
purposes of specific makings of statements; to the unsatisfied wishes of
specific audiences. No alteration in things in the world, nor any magical
replaying of the course of events, could bring statements so condemned
into line, in the way that an "exaggerated assessment" of the height of
a building could be brought into line by inorganic growth. Whether the
statement (that p) is true or false is a matter of the way things are (of
whether p) ; whether a statement is exaggerated (if the question arises—
which depends on the type of statement and the possibilities of the
language) is a matter of the way things are (e.g., of whether or not
there were fewer than 2,000 there). But whether a statement is overconcise[14] or too general depends on what the hearer wants to know. The
world does not demand to be described with one degree of detail rather
than another.

5. THE SCOPE OF "STATEMENT," "TRUE," "FALSE," AND "FACT"

Commands and questions obviously do not claim to be statements of
fact: they are not true or false. In Section 6 of his paper, Mr. Austin
reminds us that there are many expressions neither interrogative nor imperative in form which we use for other purposes than that of reportage
or forecast. From our employment of these expressions he recommends
that we withhold (suspects that we do, in practice, largely withhold) the
appellation "stating facts," the words "true" and "false." Philosophers,
even in the sphere of language, are not legislators; but I have no wish
to challenge the restriction, in some philosophical contexts, of the words
"statement," "true," "false," to what I have myself earlier called the
"fact-stating" type of discourse.

---

[14] "Concise" is perhaps less often used of what a man says than of the way he
says it (e.g., "concisely put," "concisely expressed," "a concise formulation").
A may take 500 words to say what B says in 200. Then I shall say that B's
formulation was more concise than A's, meaning simply that he used fewer
words.

What troubles me more is Mr. Austins' own incipient analysis of this type of discourse. It seems to me such as to force him to carry the restriction further than he wishes or intends. And here there are two points which, though connected, need to be distinguished. First, there are difficulties besetting the relational theory of truth as such; second, there is the persistence of these difficulties in a different form when this "theory of truth" is revealed as, rather, an incipient analysis of the statement-making use of language.

First then, facts of the cat-on-the-mat-type are the favored species for adherents of Mr. Austin's type of view. For here we have one thing (one chunk of reality) sitting on another: we can (if we are prepared to commit the errors commented on in Section [2] above) regard the two together as forming a single chunk, if we like, and call it a fact or state of affairs. The view may then seem relatively plausible that to say that the statement (made by me to you) that the cat is on the mat is true is to say that the three-dimensional state of affairs with which the episode of my making the statement is correlated by the demonstrative conventions is of a type with which the sentence I use is correlated by the descriptive conventions. Other species of fact, however, have long been known to present more difficulty: the fact that the cat is not on the mat, for example, or the fact that there are white cats, or that cats persecute mice, or that if you give my cat an egg it will smash it and eat the contents. Consider the simplest of these cases, that involving negation. With what type of state-of-affairs (chunk of reality) is the sentence "The cat is not on the mat" correlated by conventions of description? With a mat *simpliciter?* With a dog on a mat? With a cat up a tree? The amendment of Mr. Austin's view to which one might be tempted for negative statements (i.e., "S is true" = "The state of affairs to which S is correlated by the demonstrative conventions is *not* of a type with which *the affirmative form of* S is correlated by the descriptive conventions") destroys the simplicity of the story by creating the need for a different sense of "true" when we discuss negative statements. And worse is to follow. Not all statements employ conventions of demonstration. Existential statements don't, nor do statements of (even relatively) unrestricted generality. Are we to deny that these are statements, or create a further sense of "true"? And what has become of the non-linguistic correlate, the chunk of reality? Is this, in the case of existential or general statements, the entire world? Or, in the case of negatively existential statements, an ubiquitous nonpresence?

As objections to a correspondence theory of truth, these are familiar points; though to advance them as such is to concede too much to the theory. What makes them of interest is their power to reveal how such a theory, in addition to its intrinsic defects, embodies too narrow a conception of the fact-stating use of language. Mr. Austin's description of the conditions under which a statement is true, regarded as an anlysis of the fact-stating use, applies only to affirmative subject-predicate statements, i.e., to statements in making which we refer to some one or more localized thing or group of things, event or set of events, and characterize it or them in some positive way (identify the object or objects and affix the label). It does not apply to negative, general, and existential statements nor, straightforwardly, to hypothetical and disjunctive statements. I agree that any language capable of the fact-stating use must have some devices for performing the function to which Mr. Austin exclusively directs his attention, and that other types of statements of fact can be understood only in relation to this type. But the other types *are* other types. For example, the word "not" can usefully be regarded as a kind of crystallizing-out of something *implicit* in all use of descriptive language (since no predicate would have any descriptive force if it were compatible with everything). But from this it does not follow that negation (i.e., the *explicit* exclusion of some characteristic) is a kind of affirmation, that negative statements are properly discussed in the language appropriate to affirmative statements. Or take the case of existential statements. Here one needs to distinguish two kinds of demonstration or reference. There is, first, the kind whereby we enable our hearer to identify the thing or person or event or set of these which we then go on to characterize in some way. There is, second, the kind by which we simply indicate a locality. The first (*"Tabby* has the mange") answers the question "Who (which one, what) are you talking about?" The second (*"There's* a cat") the question "Where?" It is plain that no part of an existential statement performs the first function; though Austin's account of reference-cum-description is appropriate to reference of this kind rather than to that of the other. It is clear also that a good many existential statements do not answer the question "Where?" though they may license the inquiry. The difference between various types of statements, and their mutual relations, is a matter for careful description. Nothing is gained by lumping them all together under a description appropriate only to one, even though it be the basic, type.

6. CONCLUSION

My central objection to Mr. Austin's thesis is this. He describes the conditions which must obtain if we are correctly to declare a statement true. His detailed description of these conditions is, with reservations, correct as far as it goes, though in several respects too narrow. The central mistake is to suppose that in using the word "true" we are asserting such conditions to obtain. That this is a mistake is shown by the detailed examination of the behavior of such words as "statement," "fact," etc., and of "true" itself, and by the examination of various different types of statement. This also reveals some of the ways in which "true" actually functions as an assertive device. What supremely confuses the issue is the failure to distinguish between the task of elucidating the nature of a certain type of communication (the empirically informative) from the problem of the actual functioning of the word "true" within the framework of that type of communication.

A PROBLEM ABOUT TRUTH

G. J. WARNOCK

1. The problem to which this paper[1] is addressed is a quite narrowly limited one: and it can be stated—though not, I think, solved—very briefly indeed. When somebody says something and we say 'That's true,' do we therein make some statement about a statement, some assertion about an assertion? Do we say something *about* what he has said? If we do, there may arise the question what the statement or assertion so made may mean: I shall allude to this question too, though only very sketchily.

This problem is one of the matters—there were several others—on which Austin and Strawson found themselves in disagreement in their papers in the symposium *Truth* in 1950 (*Proceedings of the Aristotelian*

---

[1] This is a rewritten and somewhat shortened version of a paper which I read first at Princeton in April 1962, and subsequently at several other places. I suspect that I have incorporated in this revised version several points which I owe to discussion with others (and no doubt I ought to have incorporated more): but, memory being both fallible and fragmentary, I cannot now do more than extend a general, though grateful, acknowledgement to those concerned.

Society, Supp. Vol. XXIV).[2] It will be convenient to take the relevant parts of that important discussion as a text from which to begin.

I should mention, perhaps, that I shall not discuss the view, which has had distinguished sponsors, that to say that something is true is to make an assertion about a sentence. Both Austin and Strawson took this view to be fairly obviously wrong, at least when the use of a natural language is in question. What can properly be said to be true or false is not a sentence itself, but rather what is, on this occasion or that, asserted, stated, said by one who utters a sentence—not the sentence he utters, but the statement he makes. This is surely correct.

2. The relevant part of Austin's account—which he took to be, so far as it goes, so obvious as to be practically truistic—was this.[3] Words, we may say generally and doubtless somewhat vaguely, are used among other things in speaking about the world, among other things in making statements about it. For this purpose, and not bringing in more complexities than are needed for the matter in hand, there must be 'two sets of conventions': (a) *descriptive* conventions correlating some words in language with 'types' of situations or states of affairs to be found in the world; and (b) *demonstrative* conventions correlating words as uttered on particular occasions with 'historic' situations or states of affairs to be found, at particular though not necessarily closely circumscribed times and/or places, in the world. 'A statement is said to be true when the historic state of affairs to which it is correlated by the demonstrative conventions (the one to which it 'refers') is of a type with which the sentence used in making it is correlated by the descriptive conventions.'

Now if the statement that S is true, then the statement that the statement that S is true is certainly itself true, and conversely: but, Austin holds, it is not the case, for this or any other reason, that the predicative phrase 'is true' is, as some have argued, 'logically superfluous,' or that to say that a statement is true is not to make any further assertion at all— any assertion, that is, other than that made by the statement itself. For (among other things) the statement that the statement that S is true is, as the statement that S usually will not be, about a statement, and in particular about the statement that S: it is therefore not the same statement as the statement that S, notwithstanding their—of course inevitable—linkage of truth-values and the fact that no doubt, in some sense or other, they convey just the same information about 'the world.' Austin's conclusion, perhaps not quite explicit but I think quite definite, is that the statement that the statement that S is true can be said to state, to mean, that the words uttered (if they were actually uttered) in making

---

[2] See above, pp. 18ff.
[3] See above, pp. 21ff.

the statement that S are correlated by demonstrative conventions with a
'historic' situation or state of affairs which is of the 'type' with which
the sentence used (if it was actually used) in making that statement is
correlated by descriptive conventions. (The point of the parentheses is
to allow for the fact that, for the statement that S to be said to be true,
it is not strictly necessary that the statement that S should actually have
been made. It may also be noted that this account is quite consistent with
the fact that the statement that S may be made at different times and
places, by different people, and in different words.) As Austin puts it in
conclusion: "If it is admitted that the rather boring yet satisfactory relation between words and world which has here been discussed does genuinely occur, why should the phrase 'is true' not be our way of describing it? And if it is not, what else is?"

To this, that part of Strawson's reply which I wish to discuss runs as
follows. Let us allow—though in fact he has substantial reservations of
detail—that, when a true statement is made, certain words are in fact
related to the world in the ways Austin describes. It is nevertheless completely mistaken, a mistake in principle, to suppose that one who says
that a statement is true means, or asserts, that the words are thus related to the world, that he is stating this *about* the statement made. Austin
has answered (perhaps and up to a point) the question *when,* in what
circumstances or conditions, we use the phrase 'is true'; but he is quite
wrong in assuming, as he evidently does, that this answers the question
how we use it. And in fact, if we consider realistically the question how
we use it, we see that we use it in a quite wide variety of ways—in expressing agreement or assent, for instance, in accepting, admitting, corroborating, endorsing, conceding, or confirming what is or might be said.
Such a remark as 'That's true' is perhaps, in some bald and uninterest-
ing grammatical sense, 'about' a statement: but its actual use is not significantly different from that of other such agreement-expressing devices
as 'Yes,' 'I quite agree,' 'You're right,' or even a nod of the head—
none of which, of course, could be supposed for a moment to be employed in making a statement about a statement, or an assertion about
the relations of certain words to the world. All these locutions and devices are appropriately used *when* a statement has been made; but it is
quite wrong to suppose that any is genuinely used to say something
about the statement.

3. In his paper, and particularly in this part of his paper, Strawson
has been taken by some to be propounding what I have heard called 'the
performative theory of truth': but I think it is clear that what he says
neither deserves, nor surely claims, any such title. It is indeed by no

means perfectly clear what a 'theory of truth' is, what is sought to be achieved by the construction of a theory so-called: but it is sufficiently clear, I believe, that Strawson has not constructed one. For a 'theory of truth' would presumably have to aspire to throw some sort of light on contexts in general in which 'true' or 'truth' might occur, or in which questions of truth or falsehood might arise: whereas Strawson's observations, as they stand, could have application only to occurrences of 'true' as a predicate in indicative sentences whose grammatical subjects refer, in one way or another, to statements. The word 'true' may also occur in, for instance, interrogative or optative or conditional sentences; and whatever its 'performative' function in such settings may be, it can scarcely be that of expressing agreement (etc.). The fact is, I take it, that just as Austin had addressed himself primarily to the particular case in which some statement, what someone says, is (indicatively) said to be true, so Strawson does not attempt to describe quite in general how we use the *word* 'true'; he accepts in effect a similar restriction, to uses of the *phrase* 'is true' as a predicate in indicative sentences. It would in fact be perfectly reasonable to suppose that these uses are fundamental; and in any case, even if such a relatively restricted discussion can scarcely issue in so high-sounding a thing as a 'theory of truth,' there is probably no harm in accepting the restriction.

We have to consider, then, these sharply different and seemingly conflicting accounts of such a locution as, for instance, 'That's true.' And first of all it is necessary to raise the question whether they actually are conflicting. It has been, I think, much too easily taken for granted that they are.

With Strawson's view that to say 'That's true' may be, for instance, to express agreement with what someone has said, it is, of course, impossible to disagree: it is quite obvious that that is so, that this is at least one of the ways in which 'is true' is used. But does it follow that to say 'That's true' is not to make a statement *about* what someone has said? Plainly not. For just as I may, say, insult or express hostility to someone by making about him the statement that he is a fool, so surely I might express agreement with what someone has said by making about what he has said the statement that it is true. Agreeing, endorsing, etc., surely do not, any more than criticizing, insulting, etc., exclude the making of a statement: for they may all be done *by* the making of a statement. Again, if someone were to say, correctly, that the phrase 'is a fool' is often used to criticize, belittle, denigrate, or insult the person of whom it is predicated, it is plain that he would not have offered an answer to the question what the phrase 'is a fool' *means:* and similarly, it would seem that one who says, correctly, that 'is true' is often used to indicate the speaker's agreement has offered no answer to the quite different question, what the words 'is true' mean.

Thus, from the fact that Strawson is most undoubtedly correct in saying that the phrase 'is true' is used—as are several other equally handy expressions—to express agreement, to accept, confirm, corroborate, etc., it does not follow *either* that to say 'That's true' is not to make a statement, *or* that there may not well arise the, as yet quite unanswered, question what the meaning of the phrase 'is true' may be. Thus, for holding that Austin is mistaken 'in principle' in supposing that 'is true' is a predicative phrase commonly employed in making statements about statements, and that its meaning is to be elucidated in terms of some relation between words and world, some quite other ground is required than merely that Strawson is correct in saying that the phrase is used, as are others, in for instance expressing agreement. It is really pretty plain that Austin was not attempting to deny this fact and had not overlooked it, but supposed that it left entirely untouched those different issues with which he himself was primarily concerned: and this supposition looks, on the face of it, entirely reasonable.

4. If then one must find, as I think one obviously must, some other ground for the view that Austin's account is in principle a mistaken one, what other ground might one adduce? I think that what Strawson's argument requires, and what in some measure his paper actually contains, is an attempt to assimilate 'the use' of the locution 'That's true' to the use of such other locutions as 'Yes,' 'You're right,' 'I quite agree,' and so on—an attempt, that is, to show that while the locution 'That's true' has, as it has undeniably, the grammatical air of a statement-making locution, this air is not to be taken seriously as a guide to its 'use.' This might run somewhat as follows:

Suppose that it is raining heavily, and that persons A, B, C, D, and E can see that it is: and suppose that A makes the statement that it's raining heavily. B then says 'Yes': C says 'It is indeed': D says 'I quite agree': and E says 'That's true.' Now certainly the responses of B, C, D, and E are verbally diverse; 'Yes,' I dare say, is not a sentence at all, and the other three sentences have quite different subjects and predicates. But —Strawson might argue—would it not be scholastic and indeed misguided to attach much significance to this verbal diversity? For surely what B, C, D, and E have in mind in responding to A's observation, what they wish to convey, what they are up to, their point, is in each case exactly the same—namely, they wish simply to indicate their agreement with or acceptance of A's remark about the state of the weather. Now it is quite plain that to say 'Yes' or 'It is indeed' or 'I quite agree' is not to make a statement about a statement; and it is no less plain that to say 'That's true' is, in intention and general effect, equivalent to, a mere conversational variant upon, saying 'Yes' or 'It is indeed' or 'I quite agree.' But if so, to hold, as Austin evidently does, that to say 'That's true' is something quite different in character and meaning from saying any of these other things, is surely to attach excessive weight to, and so to be led astray by, mere surface grammar. The *use* of these locutions, which is what really counts, is exactly the same; and there is no more reason seriously to suppose that one who says 'That's true' is making a statement about a statement than there would be to suppose this of one who says 'So it is.' The fact is simply that both, in verbally diverse formulas, would be (for instance) expressing their agreement with what was said.

This, I think, is not unpersuasive. It seems indeed pretty undeniable that one who says conversationally 'That's true' will often mean nothing more than, at any rate in the sense that he has in mind nothing different from, one who may say, for instance, 'I agree.' But here there naturally arises a question: how does it come about, one may well wish to ask, that we should have available for the single purpose of, say, expressing agreement, this rather large number of verbally diverse formulas? If, as the view just outlined evidently implies, their verbal diversity is of no serious significance, does it not seem that we are confronted here with a curious kind of linguistic superabundance, a surprising superfluity of ways of doing just the same thing? How is such linguistic prodigality to be accounted for?

Now surely an explanation of this circumstance comes readily to mind. It must be remembered that although, of course, we speak for the most part with the effortless ease born of years of practice, in fact the making of even a quite simple statement is a performance of some considerable complexity. In saying to me truly, for instance, 'It's raining heavily,' you have, intending to comment on current weather conditions in our vicinity, correctly produced exactly that utterance best adapted in our common language to this very purpose: you have not only successfully drawn my attention to the place and time intended, but have also characterized correctly the relevant aspect or feature of what is going on there and then. Now suppose that, on observing your performance, I wish to express no dissent, that I have no criticism to offer of any of the several aspects of your complex undertaking. Well, there is a simple formula available to me, specially designed for letting you know in a single word of my nondissent; I can say 'Yes.' More formally, but just as well, I can indicate my nondissent in the formula 'I quite agree.' Alternatively, I can as it were commend you for your faultless performance and the correctness of your views; I can say 'You're right.' Or again, concentrating on the point that the state of the weather in our vicinity is indeed just as you say it is, I can respond with 'It is indeed.' But there is yet one further possibility; I can, not directly alluding to you, to your performance, or to the weather, advert to the point that what was said by you in uttering the words you uttered was, as these matters are conventionally understood, such as to designate a particular state of the weather which is further, as these matters are conventionally understood, of just that type for the characterization of which the words used were perfectly appropriate. I can, in short, say 'That's true.'

Now are all these verbally diverse responses 'used in the same way'? Well, in a sense no doubt they are. They all have the same general object and serve the same purpose; for they all serve to let you know of my total nondissent. Whichever of these things I choose, or more probably just happen, to come out with, you know that I am with you on the question of what the state of the weather is. Are they then indistinguishable (except trivially, as words)? Surely not. For is it not evident that, notwithstanding their identity of general object, they achieve this single object in quite different ways, by responding to or commenting on different parts, features, or aspects of the whole rather complex performance of stating truly that it's raining heavily? The reason why there are many ways of doing just the same thing, of achieving just the same general object, is that the making of a statement has many sides to it; there are many points at which, and hence many devices by which, our nondissent (or of course our dissent) may be indicated. But if so, does it not seem perfectly evident that what distinguishes 'That's true' from the rest is that it, and it alone, says something *about* what the speaker said, *about* the statement he made? 'Yes' does no such thing, nor yet do 'I agree' and 'You're right': these serve the purpose every bit as well, but not in the same way. Just so I may, say, congratulate an orator by saying 'I congratulate you' or 'That was an excellent speech': and the fact that in either case I congratulate the orator does not imply that these remarks are not significantly distinguishable, or that the second does not differ from the first by being, among other things, *about* the speech that he made.

5. This might be objected to. It might be held, with some justice, that a certain air of artificiality attaches to the above discussion of diverse responses to 'It's raining heavily.' Can it seriously be suggested that, for instance, one who says 'You're right' conceives himself to be, has in mind that he is, saying something about the speaker, as distinguished from one who, in saying 'That's true,' says something about what the speaker said, or from one who, in saying 'I agree,' says nothing about either? No such distinctions, surely, are in any degree likely to be in such a speaker's

mind. What was called the 'general object' of all the responses considered —namely, indication of agreement with what the first speaker said—is likely to be *all* that respondents in such a case have in mind. But if so, what serious sense can be attached to the claim that one who happens to say 'That's true' is to be *distinguished* as therein making a statement about what was said?

But this objection, I believe, rests too much weight on the question of what speakers may have in mind, on what they may consciously conceive themselves to be doing, and correspondingly too little on what may be called the mechanism of language itself. Wittgenstein in particular laid great and justified stress on the idea that the understanding of an expression, the grasp of what (in one sense at least) it means, does not particularly require, and may even be obstructed by, attention to what passes in the mind of one who uses it when he does so. Similarly, I think, the question of what a speaker is doing in speaking—a question, we may note, that in most cases can be taken and answered in several different ways—is not to be conclusively answered by reference to what he conceives himself to be doing, or to what he has it in mind to do. One thing that a speaker does who says 'It's raining heavily' is, for instance, to utter a sentence in grammatical English, and this may even be essential to his being understood by his hearers: but is it likely that, and does it at all matter whether, the notion of uttering a sentence in grammatical English was ever actually in his mind?

Or consider an example somewhat closer to the question now at issue. In certain circles, in certain parts of the world, agreement with statements made is not uncommonly expressed in the colloquial formula 'You can say that again'; and it may well be the case that one who utters these words will, if this idiom is very familiar to him, have nothing whatever in mind in uttering them but the intention of indicating his agreement with what has been said. Nevertheless, it is surely undeniable that what the words actually mean is that the person addressed has leave, or is at liberty, to repeat the observation he has just made: and to utter the words is to tell him that this is so. Could we not hold then, somewhat analogously, that whereas Strawson probably describes correctly enough what ordinary users of the words 'That's true' very often, or typically, have in mind in using them, Austin is not thereby any less entitled to offer his observations in answer to two quite different questions—first, what the words 'That's true' actually mean, and second, what speech-act is standardly performed in uttering those words?

This looks well enough, perhaps; and it has about it a pleasingly pacificatory air; but it is not yet, I think, quite plain sailing. It might be urged, for instance, that I have just appealed to a misleading analogy.

It is certainly a feature of the case just cited that, while the words 'You can say that again' colloquially have, in certain circles, this mere agreement-indicating role, the same words may and no doubt often do occur in quite other contexts. A colleague confides to me, for example, that he made a very gratifying impression in his lectures last term with the remark 'Santayana was the Puccini of philosophy': how, he asks me, can he enjoy a similar success this term? I, knowing perhaps that few people attend my colleague's lectures more than once, might then quite naturally point out the path to another triumph by saying 'You can say that again': and here, while not necessarily endorsing his rather complex assessment of Santayana, I do literally tell him that it is open to him to repeat the dictum in question. But did the plausibility of our distinction between what the speaker has in mind in speaking, and the meaning of his words or the nature of the speech-act performed, not derive perhaps from this undoubted distinction between colloquial and standard uses of 'You can say that again'? If these words had occurred *only* in their agreement-indicating role, it would surely have been scarcely possible to distinguish *from* this the meaning of the words, or what is done by one who utters them. What then of the locution 'That's true'? Is this properly analogous with 'You can say that again'?

Well, the answer seems clearly to be that the analogy is not perfect: but the respect in which it fails tends, I believe, substantially to strengthen Austin's case. The words 'You can say that again,' we said, have a *colloquial* role, namely as a mere indication of the speaker's agreement: this is colloquial—or perhaps idiomatic?—in the sense that this role for the words in question is not a mere standard function of their standard meanings, or a standard extension of their standard uses: a foreigner, for instance, well schooled in classical English, would probably not be able straight off to construe their utterance correctly. The locution 'That's true' is certainly not in this position: for it is in no way at all, of course, colloquial or idiomatic. But this is to say—and this begins to seem perfectly obvious—that the use of those words to express agreement (etc.) *is* an entirely standard function of their standard meaning: that, in fact, the reason why one who says 'That's true' can be taken to have expressed his agreement with what was said, is simply that he has said *about* what was said that it is true, and to say this about what was said can be, simply in virtue of what the word 'true' standardly means, to express agreement with it. Whereas, in the case of the words 'You can say that again,' we found a (colloquial) agreement-indicating role and *also* a standard use of the words to tell somebody something, we seem to find, in the case of 'That's true,' a (noncolloquial) agreement-indicating role *because of* what is meant by the words and done by one who utters them. But if so, some such account of them as Austin offers appears not as an incompatible rival to, but rather as the essential underlying rationale of, such an account as Strawson's. It is precisely *because,* as Austin says, one who says 'That's true' therein makes a certain statement about a statement that, as Strawson says, he thereby expresses (for instance) his agreement with it.

At the same time, it would, no doubt, be most ill-advised to offer 'That's true' as a central or ideal instance of statement-making. For one thing, it has the peculiarity that it will often, perhaps more often than not, be addressed to someone who already knows or believes it, and has indeed, by making the statement referred to, given recent evidence of his knowledge or belief. The statement 'That's true' will only convey to the person to whom it is addressed information about its subject matter if that person either did not make, and did not know to be true, the statement referred to, or—a queer case—made the statement but did not know whether it was true or not. Thus the dialectical function, so to speak, of the utterance 'That's true' is somewhat peculiar: it will not usually be primarily to convey what it actually states, but rather to convey what its making incidentally implies—namely, that the utterer believes, accepts, agrees with (etc.) the statement which his utterance is about. For this same reason it is also the case, no doubt, that one who makes the statement 'That's true' will often not have *particularly* in mind the idea that he is making a statement at all: the point of his statement will be primarily to convey his agreement (etc.), and that he is doing this may well be all that he has in mind. However, although such considerations as these well warrant the conclusion that the utterance 'That's true' is a somewhat unideal specimen of statement-making, they do not seem to me to be adequate grounds for the denial that it is a case of statement-making at all.

6. This conclusion can now be reinforced, I believe, if we reconsider the matter of 'the use' of such verbally diverse locutions as 'Yes,' 'I quite agree,' 'You're right,' 'That's true,' and so on. Now it is certainly the case, as Strawson insists, that there are contexts in which any of these could be used indifferently: if, for instance, you have observed to me that it's raining heavily and I wish to let you know of my nondissent, that job will be done perfectly by the utterance of any of these locutions. But is this to say that they are all 'used in the same way'? Plainly not. For—apart from the question whether, even in such a context as this, they may be distinguishable—the conclusion that they are 'used in the same way' would seem to require, not only that there should be contexts in which they are indifferently interchangeable but also that there should be no

contexts in which they are not. But this latter condition is surely, and significantly, not satisfied.

Let us consider, for instance, the case of agreement. I may, certainly, agree with a statement that someone has made. But not, of course, *only* with statements. I may also agree with a decision he has come to, a policy he has announced, a taste or opinion he has expressed, an appraisal, an estimate, or an assessment he has made. He says, for instance, concluding his argument, '. . . so we must try to get Jones elected instead of Smith,' or '. . . on those grounds I judge Higgins to be the more promising man.' Now if I agree with his decision or his assessment, I may of course say 'Yes, I agree': if I believe his decision or assessment to be correct, I may say 'You're right.' But in neither case, surely, would I naturally, or could I properly, say 'That's true.' *This* way of expressing agreement would be quite out of place here. Why? Because, presumably, the speaker with whose words I wish to signify my agreement was not just making a statement, purveying a simple truth (or falsehood), but rather announcing a decision, issuing an appraisal: and though indeed I may agree with him and may express my agreement, the particular form of words 'That's true' seems properly, and also naturally though doubtless not rigorously, to be confined to the particular case in which what is to be agreed with is, or at least is offered and taken as, a statement of fact. Thus, in these and no doubt in vastly many other cases, it appears that our various agreement-expressing locutions are *not* in fact freely interchangeable: though there are cases in which any would do, there are other cases in which one or more will do, while others will not.

But now, of course, the question arises: why should it be the case, as it appears to be, that the locution 'That's true' is naturally, though doubtless neither rigorously nor self-consciously, confined to the case in which what is to be agreed with is a statement of fact? Is this a mere convention of speech, like the use of 'Hear, hear' by way of assent to formal oratory, or of 'Amen' as a mark of subscription to the sentiments of a prayer? It is surely both unplausible and unnecessary to suppose that this is a mere convention. For it seems at this point both natural and quite adequately explanatory to hold that to say 'That's true' is to say, about what someone has said, that it is true; so that *of course* one can express agreement in this particular form of words only if what one is thereby talking about is the kind of thing that *can* be true (or untrue)— that is, is a statement. Thus, the notion that to say 'That's true' is to make a statement about a statement appears not only not to be ruled out by the point that that utterance may serve to express agreement, but actually to be indispensably necessary to understanding of the restrictions on the expression of agreement in that particular form. That—more or less—only statements can be agreed with in this way is explained if the utterance *states, about* what it refers to, that it is true; and I cannot imagine how else that fact is to be explained.

7. One final point. I believe that many people have been inclined to object that, even if one is led by the sort of considerations outlined above to the view that Austin is probably right in holding that one who says 'That's true' makes a statement about a statement, there is still grave difficulty in accepting his implicit view that the statement so made *means* anything so lengthy and elaborate as he says it does. For, one may think, it is surely quite indisputable that those simple and unreflective persons who say 'That's true,' quite naturally and effortlessly, dozens of times a day, do not have any such lengthy rigmarole—about demonstrative and descriptive conventions and so on—in mind when they say it. I do not believe, however, that there is much force in this objection. For one thing, there is a high degree of indeterminacy in the notion of meaning (some of it, indeed, perhaps put there by philosophers); so that it is very far from clear what kind of account, how thoroughgoing and far-reaching and how elaborate, of the use or conditions of application of a term can properly be put forward as an account of its meaning. But more generally, there is surely no good reason to believe that a philosophically useful account of 'the meaning' of a term must not be more complex than, or even that it must bear any very close relation to, what ordinary users of the term may have in mind when they use it. It is, after all, a very familiar point that those who habitually use a term quite correctly, and in that sense may be said to know what it means, may be in hopeless difficulties when invited to *say* what it means: and it seems clear that, when an attempt to say what it means is seriously undertaken, the resulting account will very often be of a complexity unsuspected by, and perhaps astonishing to, plain speakers of the language. Thus, whatever objections there may be to Austin's account of what it means to say of a statement that it is true, I do not believe that the undoubted complexity of his account is in itself a ground for the conclusion that it must be incorrect.

My argument, then, can be summed up as follows:

(1) Though it is most undoubtedly the case that, when one says 'That's true,' one is often, for instance, agreeing, it does not follow from this that one is not therein making a statement: for one may express agreement *by* making a statement.

(2) It is quite certainly the case that, as Strawson says, one may express, say, agreement with somebody's statement more or less indiffer-

ently by saying 'That's true,' 'So it is,' 'I agree,' 'Yes,' 'You're right,' and so on. But:

(3) It appears *not* to be the case that, as he implies, these verbally diverse responses cannot be significantly and substantially distinguished from one another. For (a) if we bring into view the actual complexity of the business of making even a quite simple statement, it at once seems natural to distinguish these diverse responses as relating to different aspects of or elements in that complex business, notwithstanding the fact that they all achieve the same general object: and the response 'That's true' is naturally seen as differing from the others in being *about* the statement made, what the speaker said. And (b) if we note that the phrases mentioned in (2) above are, though freely interchangeable in some contexts, not so interchangeable in others, we observe that 'That's true' tends to be restricted to contexts in which it is statements of fact that are, say, to be agreed with: and it seems the obvious explanation of this restriction that 'That's true' states, about what its subject-term refers to, that it is true.

(4) It appears in general not outrageous to hold that one who utters certain words therein makes a statement about something, even if he does not clearly and self-consciously conceive himself to be so doing: though

(5) We may well regard saying 'That's true' in the ordinary way as, though in no way deviant or colloquial or idiomatic, yet a somewhat unideal specimen of making a statement.

(6) If we hold, then, with Austin, that to say 'That's true' is to make a statement, albeit perhaps an unideal one, about a statement, we may still feel difficulty in the idea that that statement's meaning can be so complicated as he makes it out. But this is far from conclusive, since there is actually no good reason why a remark, perhaps made very casually, with nothing very complex in mind, should not all the same, when subjected to scrutiny, turn out to have a highly complex meaning, only to be set out in perhaps surprisingly many hard words.

In this paper I have not, of course, done anything whatever to show that Austin's account of *what* is stated about a statement, when one says that it is true, is in detail correct. If I have established anything, it is only that Strawson does not succeed in showing that an account of that kind is in principle wrong—that is, that Austin goes astray in principle in supposing that to say 'That's true' is to make *any* kind of assertion about a statement. I am in fact inclined to believe not only that Strawson does not show this to be wrong in principle, but also that it *is* not wrong in principle: but of course this is not to say that Austin's account is wholly acceptable as it stands,[4] still less that there do not remain far more questions than it answers.

---

[4] It may be worth pointing out two curious, but not I think very important, slips which Austin's paper contains. First, he says at one point that "the relation between the statement that S and the world which the statement that the statement that S is true asserts to obtain is a *purely conventional* relation . . ." But this, which Strawson rightly objects to, is not a consequence of Austin's account but actually inconsistent with it. On his own view, all that is 'purely conventional' is that to utter the sentence 'S' is to make the statement that S: whether or not the statement so made is true is of course a matter not of convention, but of fact. Second, he says that 'demonstrative' conventions correlate 'the words (= statements) with the historic situations, etc., to be found in the world.' But again, on his own view, that a particular *statement* relates to a particular 'historic' situation is a matter not of convention, nor in this case of fact, but of logic: for he implies earlier that a statement is identified, in part, by reference to the situation to which it relates. What 'demonstrative conventions' in part determine is not how statements are related to the world, but what statement is made by the utterance of certain words on a particular occasion. It will be noted that I have sought to eliminate this latter slip in my initial brief statement of Austin's view.

A PROBLEM ABOUT TRUTH—
A REPLY TO MR. WARNOCK

I

The point on which Mr. Warnock principally insists in his paper is that someone who says that a certain statement is true thereby makes a statement about a statement. The point is not one that I shall dispute; and since it will be convenient to have a name for it, I shall refer to it as the undisputed thesis. The importance of the undisputed thesis appears to Mr. Warnock to lie in the bearing it has on attempts to answer, or on criticisms of attempts to answer, certain philosophically debated questions. These questions, as alluded to by Mr. Warnock at various points in his paper, can be distinguished (or, perhaps, grouped) as follows:

(1) What is done (or what speech-act is standardly performed) by one who says that a statement is true?

(2) What is meant (or what is asserted) by a statement (or by someone who states) that a statement is true?

(3) What is the meaning of the word 'true' (or of the phrase 'is true' or of the phrase 'That's true')?

About (1) I shall say no more. In accepting the undisputed thesis I am clearly committed to agreeing that at least part of what anyone does who says that a statement is true is to make a statement about a statement. With the *differences* between (2) and (3) we need not be much concerned. For Mr. Warnock makes it very clear that he is mainly interested in such interpretations of (2) as would bind acceptable answers to (2) very closely to acceptable answers to (3). (He is not, for example, primarily concerned about what one who says that a statement is true may 'have in mind' in doing so.) I shall follow him in this.

A main part of Mr. Warnock's purpose, then, is to insist that no answer to the questions at (2) and (3), and no criticism of any such answer, is acceptable if that answer or criticism is incompatible with the undisputed thesis. The undisputed thesis imposes, as it were, an adequacy condition which must be satisfied by any acceptable view on these matters. This adequacy condition I shall accept.

Now Mr. Warnock certainly does not regard acceptance of this condition as counting decisively in favor of any one philosophical view about the correct answers to questions at (2) and (3). But I think it is true that he does regard acceptance of this condition as *removing an obstacle* to acceptance of such a view as Austin appeared to espouse[1] about the correct answers to these questions and also as *constituting an obstacle* to acceptance of any view of a certain apparently strongly contrasting type which I can indicate by saying that views of this type are often associated (rightly or wrongly) with the name of Ramsey and (happily or unhappily) with some such description as "the 'assertive redundancy' thesis about the meaning of 'true.' " It is at this point that I shall differ from Mr. Warnock. I shall argue that acceptance of the undisputed thesis does not favor an Austin-type as opposed to a Ramsey-type view. I shall also suggest that, insofar as they might be regarded as competitors, Mr. Warnock is himself committed to preferring a Ramsey-like to an Austinian view. Finally—for there is something absurd about the continuation of this appearance of vast disagreement—I shall suggest that we do not really here have conflicting views on one and the same question, but views which, where they overlap, agree and, where they differ, do not overlap. If the areas of difference do not overlap, they are, however, adjacent; and the *Theory of Truth* is perhaps a title ample and generous enough to accommodate beneath it a number of discussions in different, though adjacent, areas.

---

[1] See above, pp. 18ff.

II

Before we consider exactly what restrictions on philosophical analysis are imposed by the undisputed thesis, it is worth remarking that the thesis is capable of being generalized in two different directions and is indeed perhaps already implicitly generalized by Mr. Warnock in one of them. The thesis as we have it is that someone who states that a certain statement is true thereby *makes a statement* about a statement. Mr. Warnock would presumably be equally willing to insist on the parallel thesis that someone who asks whether a certain statement is true thereby *asks a question* about a statement; that one who expresses a doubt as to whether a certain statement is true thereby *expresses a doubt* about a statement; that one who advances the hypothesis that a certain statement is true thereby *advances a hypothesis* about a statement; and so on. Perhaps the generalization of the thesis in this direction can be expressed as follows: one who says anything at all by uttering a sentence which is or contains a clause within which 'is true' is predicated of a statement is thereby talking about (saying something about) a statement. This allows for the clause in question being a main assertoric or interrogative clause; or one of two disjoined clauses; or a conditional clause; or any other kind of coordinate or subordinate clause. A slightly modified way of expressing the generalization would be this: anyone who says anything such that, in the course of his saying it, the phrase 'is true' is predicated, assertorically or conditionally or in any other way, of a statement is thereby talking about (saying something about) a statement. Or, more shortly: in any predication of 'is true' of a statement, something is said, though not necessarily asserted, about a statement. Mr. Warnock does not, even implicitly, generalize the undisputed thesis in this direction; but it seems almost certain that he would be willing to do so.

Now let us consider the other possible direction of generalization. Here the issues involved are a little more complicated and Mr. Warnock's intentions are not perhaps wholly clear. We have first to ask a question about Mr. Warnock's use of the word 'statement' in the phrase 'says that a statement is true' and in the phrase 'says something about a statement.'

Consider the following cases (which may be thought of as quite unrelated to each other):

(1) Person A states, or asserts, that *p*
(2) Person B conjectures that *q*
(3) It becomes clear, without C's actually saying so, that person C holds on a certain matter the view that *r*.

In each case a comment involving the predication of 'is true' is made by some person other than A, B or C respectively. For simplicity's sake we will allow the comments to take the form of assertions in each case. The comments are:

(1) A's statement is true
(2) B's conjecture is true
(3) The view which C holds on this matter is true.

It seems quite clear that Mr. Warnock would hold, and would be right in holding, that the person who makes comment (1) is making a statement about a statement (viz., the statement that p). What is not quite so clear is whether he would also hold that each of the persons who make comments (2) and (3) is likewise making a statement about a statement (about the statement that q and about the statement that r respectively).

There are some indications in Mr. Warnock's paper, though they are not decisive indications, that he *would* hold this. For instance, he remarks, in effect, in one place[2] that it is not necessary, for the statement that p to be said to be true, that anyone should actually have *stated* that p; and he *seems* in another place[3] to treat 'x is the kind of thing that can be true (or untrue)' as equivalent to 'x is a statement.' Let us assume, first, that he really intends this equivalence and that he is using the word 'statement' unequivocally throughout. It will be well to distinguish this use of the word; and I shall do so by always writing the word, when so used, with an initial capital letter and by generally following it, when so used, with the word 'proposition' in parentheses; for the word 'proposition' has often been used by philosophers to stand quite generally for the kind of thing which can be true or untrue (the kind of thing of which 'is true' can properly be predicated) even though their explanations of this use of it have usually been confused or mistaken and have sometimes been encumbered with regrettable accretions of theory.

Now from the assumption just made about Mr. Warnock's intentions and practice, two important consequences seem to follow regarding the undisputed thesis. The first is that it is already fully generalized in the second direction I am considering. Since any significant predication of 'is true' is a predication of it of a Statement (proposition), we can simplify our previous and, as it seemed, only partially generalized reform ulation of the undisputed thesis by dropping from it what is now a redundant phrase. Instead of writing "In any predication of 'is true' *of a statement,* something is said (though not necessarily asserted) about a statement," we can write: "In any predication of 'is true,' something is said (though not necessarily asserted) about a Statement (proposition)."

---

[2] See above, p. 56.
[3] See above, p. 64.

The second consequence of this assumption regarding Mr. Warnock's intentions is perhaps a little less obvious and a little less definite. It seems likely, however, that if we do make this assumption, the conditions imposed upon philosophical analysis by acceptance of the undisputed thesis will be rather less exacting than if we make the contrary assumption. To explore this possibility we will now consider the consequences of making the contrary assumption. That is, we will consider the consequences of interpreting the phrase 'makes a statement about a statement' in such a way that the person who makes comment (1) above certainly *is* making a statement about a statement whereas the persons who make comments (2) and (3) are not, or need not be, making statements about statements, though they certainly *are* making statements about, respectively, a conjecture and a view. If the phrase is interpreted in this way— and it must be admitted to be a natural way of interpreting it—then the interpretation of the undisputed thesis is correspondingly affected. It cannot be regarded as a thesis already generalized in the direction we are now considering. It can be regarded, however, as a member of a *set* of theses such that other members of the set can be obtained from this member by substituting such words as 'conjecture,' 'view,' 'suggestion,' etc. for the word 'statement' in the formula we already have, i.e., in the formula, "In any predication of 'is true' of a statement, something is said, though not necessarily asserted, about a statement."

Why do I say that on this interpretation the undisputed thesis is likely to impose more exacting conditions than on the interpretation we considered first? It will impose more exacting conditions *if* it is insisted that the *differences* between different members of the set of theses just referred to must be reflected in any adequate analyses of different cases of predication of 'is true.' Thus suppose we have a case in which 'is true' is predicated of a conjecture and a case in which 'is true' is predicated of a statement. Then it might be held that no analysis of these predications is adequate unless the analysis reflects the fact that in one case something is said about a conjecture (rather than about, e.g., a statement) and in the other case something is said about a statement (rather than about, e.g., a conjecture). Since either of these facts entails the fact that something is said about a Statement (proposition), while the entailment does not hold conversely, this requirement is, at least formally, more stringent than the requirement that the analysis shall reflect the fact that something is said about a Statement (proposition).

I have spoken as if we (and Mr. Warnock) were obliged to choose between two interpretations of the undisputed thesis at this point. But of course this is not so; for there is no obligation to use the phrase 'saying something about a statement' unequivocally. It is open to Mr. Warnock to claim to have advanced both versions of the undisputed thesis, and it is further open to him to embrace all the members of the set of theses of which the potentially more exacting version of the undisputed thesis is a member. That is to say, Mr. Warnock can hold both:

(1) the thesis that in all predications of 'is true,' something is said about a Statement (proposition), and

(2) all members of the set of theses to which belongs the thesis that in all predications of 'is true' in which 'is true' is predicated of a statement, something is said about a statement.

Indeed, though it would be possible for someone to *advance* the thesis referred to at (1) without actually *advancing* any of the theses referred to at (2) (and conversely), it would, I think, be very difficult with any plausibility to *accept* the thesis referred to at (1) while *rejecting* the theses referred to at (2) (and conversely). So I shall assume that Mr. Warnock is willing to embrace both versions of the undisputed thesis, that is, that he is willing to embrace both (1) the thesis that in *all* predications of 'is true' something is said about a Statement (proposition) and (2) the thesis that in all predications of 'is true' in which 'is true' is predicated of a statement, something is said about a statement. This leaves me still uncertain whether he *also* wishes to insist on the more exacting requirement, which, as we've seen, can be derived from thesis (2), regarding any philosophical analysis of predications of 'is true' in which 'is true' is predicated of a statement. I shall, however, make things as difficult as possible for myself by assuming that he does intend to insist on the more exacting requirement which can be derived from thesis (2); and I shall accept this requirement, too, as imposing adequacy conditions on philosophical analysis or explication of predications of 'is true' in which 'is true' is predicated of a statement.

Before we proceed, perhaps one more word is called for about the relations between 'saying something about a Statement (proposition)' and 'saying something about a statement.' Anyone who says something about a statement (= what is stated by someone) or about a conjecture (= what is conjectured by someone) or about a belief (= what is believed by someone) *thereby* says something about a Statement (proposition). The relation this way is clear enough. But, further, any Statement (proposition) is a potential, if not an actual, statement; a potential, if not an actual, conjecture; a potential, if not an actual, belief. And we *may* use the phrase 'the belief that *p*' without implying that anyone ever believed or will believe that *p* (and without implying the contrary) and we *may* use the phrase 'the statement that *p*' without implying that anyone ever stated or will state that *p* (and without implying the contrary); and yet we may not *quite* intend in so using these phrases to use them altogether in the neutral sense of 'the Statement (proposition) that *p*.'

And then we may be inclined to say that anyone who says something about the Statement (proposition) that *p* *thereby* says something about the belief that *p*, about the conjecture that *p*, about the statement that *p*, about the judgment that *p* and so on. But if we wish to keep in the field the potentially more exacting version of the undisputed thesis, we must distinguish between the sense of the phrase 'says something about the statement that *p*' in which one who says something about the Statement (proposition) that *p* *thereby* says something about the statement that *p* and the sense of that phrase in which it does not follow, from the fact that someone says something about the Statement (proposition) that *p*, that he says anything about a statement, for he might have been saying something, not about a statement (something *stated* by someone) but about a conjecture (something *conjectured* by somebody). This, I repeat, is a condition we must observe if we wish to keep in the field the potentially more exacting version of the undisputed thesis. But we shall find in practice that there is no greater difficulty in complying with the formally more exacting than with the formally less exacting requirements of the undisputed thesis. Any difficulties that arise in practice arise with equal force in connection with both versions of the thesis.

III

In any predication of 'is true,' in which 'is true' is predicated of a statement, something is said about that statement. It is agreed that any acceptable account of predications of 'is true' must be compatible with this thesis. If we assume that philosophical explication of predications of 'is true' is to proceed by the old and honorable method of paraphrase or analysis,[4] then the above requirement may be expressed as follows: no analysis or paraphrase of any predication of 'is true' in which 'is true' is predicated of a statement is acceptable unless in the analysis or paraphrase of that predication something is said about that statement.

But now what about 'about'? Suppose our analysandum is 'A's statement is true.' How are we to interpret the requirement that any acceptable analysis for this analysandum must be *about* A's statement? We might say that the analysis must be about A's statement in the same sense as that in which the analysandum is about it. But this too poses problems of interpretation. Is it, e.g., supposed to exclude any sense of 'about' in which the analysandum might be said to be about A? Clearly the analysandum contains just one predicative phrase, viz., 'is true'; and clearly the unique subject of predication of this unique predicative phrase

---

[4] Not all philosophical elucidation by paraphrase would be allowed the name of 'analysis' by purists.

is A's statement. But equally clearly Mr. Warnock cannot intend the requirement about 'about' to be taken so strictly that any analysis or paraphrase is disqualified unless it too contains just one predicative phrase of which A's statement is the unique subject of predication. For this interpretation would disqualify the type of analysis he views with favor, the type suggested by Austin.

Suppose we say, rather, that for any analysis to be about some item, it is necessary and sufficient that that item should be the subject of predication of *some* predicative phrase occurring essentially in the analysis. Then we shall indeed be able to say that the Austinian analysis is about (1) the words uttered by A in making his statement and that it is about (2) those words *as* uttered by him on the occasion of his making that statement. But we shall still not be able to say that the analysis is about A's statement. Neither (1) nor (2) is to be identified with the statement (= what is stated) which is the subject of predication of 'is true' in the analysandum.[5] Reference to the statement comes essentially into the analysis only by way of *specifying* the items (1) and (2). All this is somewhat obscured in Austin's original drafting of his form of analysis; but that drafting incorporates what is either, as Mr. Warnock suggests, a slip or at least a different use of the word 'statement' from that in which every statement is a Statement, i.e., from that in which 'statement' = 'what is stated and may be said to be true or untrue.'

It is worth taking a little space to make these points clearer. I begin by reproducing, with the omission of two parentheses, Mr. Warnock's redrafting of the Austinian analysans for the case where the analysandum is 'The statement that S is true.' It runs: "The words uttered in making the statement that S are correlated by demonstrative conventions with a 'historic' situation or state of affairs which is of the 'type' with which the sentence used in making that statement is correlated by descriptive conventions."

Mr. Warnock's redrafting is not unexceptionable. It does not seem at first that there could be any difference between *the words uttered* in making the statement that S and *the sentence used* in making that statement. Why the change in style? Mr. Warnock has not made quite explicit the difference he wishes to convey. It can, I think, be made explicit by the following reformulation: "The words uttered in making the statement that S are, as uttered in making *that* statement, correlated by

---

[5] Mr. Warnock clearly recognizes that any identification of either (1) or (2) with a statement (or with a Statement) would be incorrect. For an admirably clear account of distinctions which must be drawn between a statement (= what is stated and may be said to be true or untrue) and other things with which a statement (= what is stated, etc.) is liable to be confused, see R. Cartwright, "Propositions," in *Analytical Philosophy*, R. J. Butler, ed. (Basil Blackwell & Mott, Ltd., 1962).

demonstrative conventions with a 'historic' situation or state of affairs
which is of the 'type' with which the words uttered, as uttered in making
any statement, are correlated by descriptive conventions." Alternatively,
using 'the sentence used' instead of 'the words uttered,' we could have:
"The sentence used in making the statement that S is, as used in making
that statement, correlated by demonstrative conventions with a 'historic'
situation or state of affairs with which the sentence used, as used in making *any* statement, is correlated by descriptive conventions." The phrase
'as uttered in making *any* statement' (or 'as used in making *any* statement') is put in for the sake of underlining the difference intended, but
could (and hereafter will) simply be omitted. As for the point which
Mr. Warnock intends to convey by the parenthetical phrases which I left
out in reproducing his draft, this could, I think, be more happily conveyed by prefacing the above reformulation with the words, "If on any
occasion the statement that S is actually made, then. . . ."

The analysans as we now have it has an unsatisfactorily betwixt-and-
between character which makes it a little difficult to measure directly
against the requirements of either version of the undisputed thesis. However we can easily obtain from it both a more general form and a less
general form of analysis. Let us take as our analysanda:

(a) the Statement (proposition) that *p* is true
(b) A's statement (what A stated) is true.

In (a) something is said about a proposition with nothing implied about
its having actually been stated or otherwise formulated (outside [a]) on
any occasion. In (b) something is said about a statement actually made
(about something actually stated) by person A on a certain occasion. In
formulating the Austinian analysans for each of these analysanda I shall
take the opportunity to do a little recasting in order to make the logical
structure of the analysans a little clearer.[6]

The analysans for (a) is:

There exists a 'historic' situation or state of affairs of a certain
'type' such that, if the proposition that *p* is actually formulated on
any occasion, then (i) the words used in formulating it are, *as* so
used, correlated by demonstrative conventions with that situation
and (ii) those words are correlated by descriptive conventions with
that type.

The analysans for (b) is:

There exists a 'historic' situation or state of affairs of a certain
'type' such that (i) the words uttered by A are, *as* uttered by him
on the occasion of making his statement, correlated by demonstra-

---

[6] I do not mean perfectly clear, but clear enough for present purposes.

tive conventions with that situation and (ii) those words are correlated by descriptive conventions with that type.

We may take the analysans for (b) as the one to measure against the requirements of the more formally exacting version of the undisputed thesis. Obviously it would be extravagant so to interpret those requirements that we had to declare that the analysans was *not* about A's statement. For A's statement is certainly *referred* to in the analysans although it is not a subject of predication there. It looks as though we had better allow that in a paraphrase of a predication of 'is true' of a statement, something is said about that statement if that statement is referred to in the paraphrase, even though it is not a subject of predication there.

Now the words 'is referred to,' though sometimes given a stricter meaning in philosophy, have naturally a rather indefinite meaning. So though it is clear that we have relaxed the requirements about 'about,' it is not clear how far we have relaxed them. However, if Mr. Warnock is right, it should be possible to set a reasonable limit to this relaxation which differentiates sharply between the results of an Austinian type of analysis or paraphrase of such a predication as (b) and the results of a Ramsey-like or 'assertive redundancy' type of analysis or paraphrase of such a predication. The former method should yield, while the latter method fails to yield, an analysis or paraphrase for (b) in which something is said about A's statement, in which A's statement is referred to.

It might seem at first as if this result was very easily achieved. If invited to give a swift summary of a Ramsey-like treatment of predications of 'is true,' one might at first respond with something like the following receipt. To obtain the sense of any predication of 'is true': substitute for the clause in which 'is true' is predicated an appropriate formualtion of the proposition itself of which 'is true' is predicated. If we simply follow this receipt where we can—it is, of course, one of the standard objections to the receipt that we cannot always follow it—we shall certainly not (in general) obtain a form of words which can be said, on even the most liberal interpretation of 'about,' to be about the proposition of which 'is true' was predicated. For few propositions are about themselves. More specifically, if we follow the receipt in a case, like (b), in which 'is true' is predicated of a statement, we shall certainly not (in general) obtain a form of words which can be said, on even the most liberal interpretation of 'about,' to be about the statement of which 'is true' is predicated. For few statements are about themselves.

However, it would be a great mistake to conclude at once, and merely from the citing of this receipt, that Mr. Warnock is right. The Ramsey-like receipt is but a clue to a general method of elucidating the predication of 'is true,' a method which has far greater flexibility than the mere citing of the receipt suggests. Thus it would be altogether too blind a

following of the receipt to suggest that the sense of the following predication of 'is true':

(c) A's statement, that X is eligible, is true

is given simply by the words:

X is eligible.

For we may say, entirely in the spirit of the Ramsey-like method, that it
is given, rather, by the words:

As A stated, X is eligible.

Is not one who says this saying something about A's statement? Does
he not refer to A's statement?

Now here it might be objected, but only in desperation, that whereas
in an Austinian analysans A's statement would be an object of definite
substantival reference (for the analysans would contain some such substantival expression as 'A's statement'), in the suggested Ramsey-like
explicans A's statement is *not* an object of definite substantival reference
(for the explicans contains no such expression). Here, it might be said,
is where we are to draw the line in relaxing the requirements for 'about.'
But this objection could be made only in desperation. For the stipulation
about 'about' is both arbitrary and ineffective.

First, let me illustrate its arbitrariness by means of an analogous
example. Someone might hold that no explication of predications of 'preceded,' in cases where 'preceded' is predicated of events, is adequate unless the offered explicans, like the explicandum, is a form of words in uttering which one would be saying something about events. Suppose the
explicandum is:

The coronation of the Emperor preceded the signing of the
treaty.

If we adopted an analogously restrictive requirement for 'about,' we
should have to reject as an explicans:

The Emperor was crowned before the treaty was signed

on the ground that it was not about events. But it would certainly be
quite contrary to normal usage to deny that the explicans was about just
the same events as the explicandum; and I might add, though it is not
relevant to our present concerns, that if this stipulation about 'about'
were *generally* joined to the kind of requirement about explication
which we are considering, then the scope of acceptable philosophical
analysis would be regrettably restricted.

The stipulation is not only arbitrary, it is ineffective. For it is quite
possible to frame somewhat inelegant variants on 'As A stated, X is
eligible' which *would* contain substantival expressions of the kind stipu-

lated: e.g., 'X is eligible, which is *what A stated*,' 'X is eligible—as per *A's statement*,' 'As *A's statement* has it, X is eligible,' etc.

The next probable line of objection is a familiar one in discussions of the Ramsey-like treatment of predications of 'is true.' It runs as follows. Perhaps this treatment appears to work for cases in which, as in (c), the predication of 'is true' itself contains a formulation of the proposition of which 'is true' is predicated. But what of cases, like (b), which contain no such formulation? What, in particular, of cases in which the person who predicates 'is true' *could* not formulate, because he does not know the content of, the propositions of which he is nevertheless able to predicate, and is perhaps prepared assertorically to predicate, 'is true'?

We must answer that such cases introduce no new difficulty of principle for a Ramsey-like treatment. For Mr. Warnock's own example, 'That's true,' we may offer 'It is as you say (state).' For (b), 'A's statement is true,' we may offer 'It is as A states' or 'It is as A says it is' or 'Things are as A says they are.' Clearly ignorance, on the part of one who predicates 'is true,' of the content of the propositions of which 'is true' is predicated makes no difference to the availability of such paraphrases as these. Consider:

(d) I don't know what the Pope is going to say, but I do know that what the Pope says is always true

(e) I don't know exactly what you're thinking, but, knowing you, I'm sure that what you're thinking isn't true.

For the relevant clause of (d) we have

. . . things are always as the Pope says they are

and for the relevant clause of (e) we have

. . . things are not as you think they are.

In general, whenever the proposition (statement or conjecture or thought) of which 'is true' is predicated is referred to, but not formulated, in the clause in which 'is true' is predicated, it will always be possible to comply with the requirements of the undisputed thesis by reproducing the substance of this reference in a clause introduced by 'as' or by some other conjunction.[7]

A curious minor point is here worth noting. Consider the case in which (1) 'is true' is predicated in a clause of the form 'it is true that p' and in which (2) the proposition that p is not therein presented as an actual statement or conjecture or thought, i.e., as one that has actually

---

[7] Thus for 'What he said about the house is true' we might have 'The house is as he said it was' or (unnaturally, but not unintelligibly) 'There is something which he said the house was and which it is.' For 'What he said about the time the last train leaves is true' we have 'The last train does leave when he said.'

been stated by someone or as a conjecture that someone has actually made or as what someone is (for certain) actually thinking. In this case, because of condition (2), the requirements of the undisputed thesis in its more exacting form might appear to be nonapplicable; and Mr. Warnock might (*might*) insist instead on the requirements of the undisputed thesis in its more general and less exacting form (i.e., he might insist that something is said, in the predication and in any satisfactory analysis of the predication, about a Statement [proposition]). The Austinian-style analysans for (a), i.e., for 'The Statement (proposition) that *p* is true,' is then available for any Austinian who wishes to offer it: i.e., the analysans which begins "There exists a 'historic' situation or state of affairs such that, if the proposition that *p* is actually formulated on any occasion, then the words used in formulating it. . . . etc." But how can the requirements of the undisputed thesis be met, in this case, on a Ramsey-like treatment? We have seen that Ramsey-like explication is not limited to blindly following that receipt which would, in this case, instruct us simply to dock the whole clause of its 'it is true that.' But what, in this case, are we to replace it by?

The answer follows from the reflection that any speaker who prefaces his formulation of the proposition that *p* by the phrase 'it is true that' under conditions such as those mentioned at (2) will normally be envisaging the proposition that *p* as something which *might* be, say, urged or objected (though by hypothesis it has not been) by some participant in the discussion. To put the point more generally. When a proposition, instead of being *merely* formulated in a clause, is also made the subject of predication of 'is true' in that clause, this is essentially because the proposition is being thought of as actually or possibly figuring in one of the many guises in which propositions may figure (e.g., as what someone states, supposes, conjectures, thinks, objects, etc.)—in addition, of course, to its so figuring in the currently framed clause. It is not, in such a case as we are considering, that there is no answer to the question in which of these guises the proposition is thought of as figuring. It is simply that a description which fits the whole class of cases gives us only a part, and only a negative part, of the answer for each one. Thus we have been told, e.g., that the proposition is *not* thought of as one which has been actually stated. But in any actual case there must be a better answer than this; and the application of the Ramsey-like treatment in any actual case is straightforward enough once the answer is known. Thus suppose our example is 'It is true that the house is an old one.' Then appropriate knowledge will enable us to paraphrase it in such a way as to meet the requirements of the undisputed thesis by some such clause as 'The house is, as you may urge (or object), an old one.' For in saying this one is referring to *what may be urged or objected* (viz., that the house is an old

one) as well as to the house. If the general point I have made about add-
ing the phrase 'it is true that' to a formulated proposition is borne in
mind, it will appear as mere bluster to insist that there must be an *invari-
ant* form of paraphrase for 'It is true that p.' We can, however, supply
the *general* form, of which any particular case will be an instance: viz.,
'As may be urged/objected/stated/thought/assumed/. . . . etc., p.'

I call this minor point a curious one because it has usually been supposed that the phrase 'it is true that p' supplies the easiest of all cases for
a Ramsey-like treatment; whereas we see that, in view of the requirements of the undisputed thesis, it in fact presents a certain *prima facie*
difficulty absent from other cases.

My conclusion, in this section, is that the requirements of the undisputed thesis do not favor an Austinian account of the sense of predications of 'is true' rather than a Ramsey-like account. If this were all
that could be established from the considerations before us, those considerations would, of course, give us no grounds for deciding between
the two accounts. But this is by no means all.

IV

What are the resemblances, and what are the differences, between the
Austinian style of paraphrase and the Ramsey-like style of paraphrase
of predications of 'is true'? Consider the resemblances. First, paraphrases
in both styles have this in common: that something is said both about
how things are in the world [8] and, if the predication of 'is true' is of a
statement, about a statement. Second—and this is extremely important—
the very thing which is said explicitly in the Ramsey-like style of paraphrase about how things are in the world and about a statement is also
said implicitly in the Austinian style of paraphrase. For in both styles of
paraphrase it is said that things in the world are as they are stated to be
by one who makes the statement. Of course, a paraphrase in the Austinian
style says more than this; but it says at least this. Now since there is
nothing in the Ramsey-like paraphrase except what it has in common
with the Austinian paraphrase, and since both paraphrases are equally
successful in dispensing with the expression 'is true,' it seems natural to
conclude that it is in virtue of what they have in common that both
paraphrases achieve this success. As far as the sense of 'is true' is concerned, then, it seems that the Austinian additions add nothing to the
Ramsey-like account.

---

[8] In the Austinian style the relevant phrase is: 'There exists a 'historic' situation of a certain type such that. . . .' In the general form of the Ramsey-like
style it is, e.g., 'Things are as. . . .'

Then how are we to understand the Austinian additions? Well, we may say that while a Ramsey and an Austin give a common answer to one question, Austin goes on to give a further answer to another. Roughly, they are at one on what it is for a (made) statement to be *true;* but Austin additionally offers a (partial) account of what it is for a (true) statement to be *made.* This is only a mnemonic. The reason for including in it the qualification 'partial' is that what Austin additionally offers is not an account of *all* the necessary conditions of a *statement's being made* but an account of *some* of the necessary conditions of a *proposition's being formulated* (expressed in words). But, of course, any necessary condition of formulating a proposition is also a necessary condition of making a statement.

To see this more clearly, let us consider a little more closely the differences between the styles of paraphrase. About the resemblances we are already clear. In the Austinian style, as in the Ramsey-like style, something is said about how things are in the world and, if the predication is of a statement, about a statement. The essential difference is that in the Austinian style something is also explicitly said, whereas in the Ramsey-like style nothing at all is explicitly said, about *words* and *semantic conventions.* A root-and-branch Austinian must maintain that these references to words and conventions are essential to explaining what is said about a statement (or, more generally, about a Statement) in any predication of 'is true' of that statement (or Statement); and he must maintain this in the face of the 'proof' just offered to the contrary. On the other hand, anyone who offers that 'proof' is under some obligation to give an alternative account of these explicit references to words and conventions. If they are not essential to elucidating the sense of 'is true,' what are they doing in the picture at all? They do not seem altogether out of place there.

Well, reference to words and conventions *is* clearly essential to elucidating what it is for a proposition to be *formulated* in any mode, assertive or other. And the Austinian formula of analysis can be simply incorporated in any such elucidatory design, as follows: a necessary (though not sufficient)[9] condition of A's formulating the proposition that p (and hence of A's making the statement that p) is that A utters words such that, if and only if p, then there is a historic situation of a certain type such that both (i) those words, as then uttered by A, are correlated by demonstrative conventions with that situation and (ii) those words are correlated by descriptive conventions with that type.

Obviously this form of (partial) analysis could be intended to apply only to empirical propositions, and scarcely seems wide enough to accom-

[9] Calling it sufficient would amount, *inter alia,* to treating all logically equivalent propositions as identical.

modate all of them (it could scarcely be held, for example, to cover scientific laws). Equally obviously, it offers no account of the differences between the various modes in which propositions may be formulated— assertoric, conditional, or other; and this may well be a merit, as clearly separating separable questions. But it is not my business now to comment on this form of analysis.[10] The point is to show that what Austin offers is not really a rival to a Ramsey-like account of the meaning of 'is true,' but a further essay in analysis in an adjacent field.

Now it is interesting to notice that Mr. Warnock, in spite of his professed sympathies, seems, at least at one point in his paper,[11] to be really of just this opinion. He criticizes Austin for what he calls the 'not very important slip' of maintaining that what is asserted in the assertion that a statement is true is the holding of certain 'purely conventional' relations between words and world. He says that Austin's *real* view (and presumably his own) is that "all that is 'purely conventional' is that to utter the sentence 'S' is to make the statement that S"; and adds: 'whether or not the statement so made *is true* is of course not a matter of convention but of fact.' By this he presumably means, not a matter of fact about conventions (unless the statement happens to be about conventions). What, then, is it a matter of fact about? Presumably a matter of fact about what the statement is about. So presumably to *say* that the statement is true is to say something about *this* matter, and also, as we have seen, about the statement—to say, in fact, that matters are as stated—and *not* to say *anything* about conventions. But, of course, if we wish, as philosophers, to go on from saying what a statement's *being true* is a matter of to saying what *making* a statement is a matter of, then we *shall* have to say something about conventions; though we shall have to mention more kinds of convention than Austin mentions, and perhaps

---

[10] It must *not* be supposed that I think it (except in the respect mentioned) free from objection. This is by no means so.

[11] See footnote, p. 67, from which my quotations come.

In this same footnote Mr. Warnock offers to correct another 'slip' of Austin's. He says that on Austin's view, as properly understood, the fact that a particular statement relates or refers to a particular 'historic' *situation* is a matter, neither of convention nor of fact, but of logic; i.e., it is a matter of the identity of the statement, of *what* statement it is. But problems arise about specifying, for a particular statement, the particular 'historic' *situation* which it is a matter of the statement's identity that it refers to. It cannot be the situation which the statement states to obtain. For this would mean that every statement was true, that it was impossible to make a false statement. Thus, if our statement is the statement that John is eligible, the situation in question cannot be the situation of John's being eligible. But, *so long as we stick to the word 'situation,'* it will not be easy to find a plausible substitute to mention as the historic item which it is a matter of the statement's identity that it refers to. Many questions arise here; but I cannot now pursue them.

to speak of other things as well, if we are to distinguish *asserting* a proposition from other modes of formulating it.

V

In the above I have not been at pains to distinguish (1) what a statement's (or Statement's) *being true* is a matter of, (2) what is meant (or
what is stated) by a statement (or by someone who states) that a certain
statement (or Statement) *is true* and (3) what the meaning (the sense)
of the phrase *'is true'* is; but have taken it that the answer to any one of
these questions carries directly with it the answer to the others. In this
I have followed Mr. Warnock. I have tried to show that he is mistaken
in suggesting that what I have called a Ramsey-like account of 'is true'
is ruled out by the requirements of the undisputed thesis; to show that
this account is an essential element in the theory Mr. Warnock views
with cautious favor; and to indicate what further questions *this* theory
may be regarded as an attempt to answer. But I have not the slightest
wish to dogmatize about what is properly included under the title of *A
Theory of Truth;* nor, once my point is conceded, to be ultimately restrictive about the meaning of "the meaning of 'is true.'" If someone
wishes to contend that we do not *really,* or do not *fully,* know the *meaning* of 'is true' unless we know what types of conventional relation obtain
between words and things when something true is stated or otherwise
expressed in words, then the contention seems to me by no means extravagant. Again, if it is maintained, as it has been, that the *real* problem of
truth is the problem of the nature of belief or of judgment; or, yet again,
that we do not *really* understand our phrase unless we know under what
conditions we are *justified* in taking something to be true (and hence,
in one sense, justified in asserting it) ; then these contentions too might
be received, at least, with sympathy. Nor is it a waste of time or irrelevant to our topic to supplement the common element in the Ramsey-like
and Austinian accounts with some discussion of the actual utility of our
phrase in common talk. Under the general title *Truth* all these matters
have, by one philosopher or another, been discussed; and since the
Ramsey-like account of the word 'true' is rather thin fare, it would seem
somewhat of a pity that so notable a title should be reserved for so
unexciting a thesis. Better, perhaps, let the theory of truth become, as it
has shown so pronounced a historical tendency to become, part of some
other theory: that of knowledge; or of mind; or of meaning.

INTRODUCTION TO
LOGICAL THEORY

P. F. STRAWSON

. . . Suppose someone says 'All John's children are asleep.' Obviously he will not normally, or properly, say this, unless he believes that John has children (who are asleep). But suppose he is mistaken. Suppose John has no children. Then is it true or false that all John's children are asleep? Either answer would seem to be misleading. But we are not compelled to give either answer. We can, and normally should, say that, since John has no children, the question does not arise. But if the form of the statement were

$$\sim(\exists x)(fx . \sim gx) \qquad \text{[Table 1]}$$

the correct answer to the question, whether it is true, would be 'Yes'; for '$\sim(\exists x)(fx)$' is a sufficient condition of the truth of '$\sim(\exists x)(fx . \sim gx)$.' And if the form of the statement were either

$$\sim(\exists x)(fx . \sim gx) . (\exists x)(fx) \qquad \text{[Table 2]}$$

or
$$\sim(\exists x)(fx . \sim gx) . (\exists x)(fx) . (\exists x)(\sim gx) \qquad \text{[Table 3]}$$

From Introduction to Logical Theory (*London: Methuen & Co., Ltd.; New York: John Wiley & Sons, Inc., 1952*). *Reprinted by permission of the author; Methuen & Co., Ltd.; and John Wiley & Sons, Inc.*

the correct answer to the question would be that the statement was false; for '$\sim(\exists x)(fx)$' is inconsistent with both these formulas. But one does not happily give either answer simply on the ground that the subject-class is empty. One says rather that the question of the truth or falsity of the statement simply does not arise; that one of the conditions for answering the question one way or the other is not fulfilled.

The adoption of any of the explicitly existential analyses, whether it be a negatively existential one (Table 1) or a conjunction of negatively and positively existential components (Tables 2 and 3), forces us to conclude that the *nonexistence* of any children of John's is sufficient to determine the truth or falsity of the general statement; makes it true for the first analysis, false for the other two. The more realistic view seems to be that the existence of children of John's is a necessary precondition not merely of the truth of what is said, but of its being *either* true *or* false. And this suggests the possibility of interpreting all the four Aristotelian forms on these lines: that is, as forms such that the question of whether statements exemplifying them are true or false is one that does not arise unless the subject-class has members.

It is important to understand why people have hesitated to adopt such a view of at least some general statements. It is probably the operation of the trichotomy 'either true or false or meaningless,' as applied to statements, which is to blame. For this trichotomy contains a confusion: the confusion between sentence and statement. Of course, the sentence 'All John's children are asleep' is not meaningless. It is perfectly significant. But it is senseless to ask, of the *sentence,* whether it is true or false. One must distinguish between what can be said about the sentence, and what can be said about the statements made, on different occasions, by the use of the sentence. It is about statements only that the question of truth or falsity can arise; and about these it can sometimes fail to arise. But to say that the man who uses the sentence in our imagined case fails to say anything either true or false is not to say that the sentence he pronounces is meaningless. Nor is it to deny that he makes a mistake. Of course, it is incorrect (or deceitful) for him to use this sentence unless (a) he thinks he is referring to some children whom he thinks to be asleep; (b) he thinks that John has children; (c) he thinks that the children he is referring to are John's. We might say that in using the sentence he *commits himself* to the existence of children of John's. It would *prima facie* be a kind of logical absurdity to say 'All John's children are asleep; but John has no children.' And we may be tempted to think of this kind of logical absurdity as a straightforward self-contradiction; and hence be led once more towards an analysis like that of Table 2; and hence to the conclusion that the man who says 'All John's children are asleep,' when John has no children, makes a false statement. But there is no need to be led, by noticing this kind of logical absurdity, towards this conclusion. For if a statement S presupposes a statement S′ in the sense that the truth of S′ is a precondition of the truth-or-falsity of S, then of course there will be a kind of logical absurdity in conjoining S with the denial of S′. This is precisely the relation, in our imagined case, between the statement that all John's children are asleep (S) and the statement that John has children, that there exist children of John's (S′). But we must distinguish this kind of logical absurdity from straightforward self-contradiction. It is self-contradictory to conjoin S with the denial of S′ if S′ is a necessary condition of the truth, simply, of S. It is a different kind of logical absurdity to conjoin S with the denial of S′ if S′ is a necessary condition of the *truth or falsity* of S. The relation between S and S′ in the first case is that S entails S′. We need a different name for the relation between S and S′ in the second case; let us say, as above, that S *presupposes* S′. . . .

A REPLY TO MR. SELLARS

P. F. STRAWSON

. . . Roughly speaking, the thesis I maintained was as follows: (a) that a statement containing[1] a definite singular description was neither true nor false unless there existed something to which the speaker was referring and which answered to the description; (b) that many statements of the kinds traditionally called universal and particular also lacked a truth-value unless there existed members of the subject-class. I shall make my qualifications mainly with reference to (a); the application to (b), where appropriate, is not difficult. The main qualification that I want to make is to admit that *in certain cases and circumstances* it may be quite natural and correct to assign a truth-value to a statement of one of these kinds (to say that it is false or even that it is true), even though the condition referred to is not satisfied. I shall begin by considering two

From "A Reply to Mr. Sellars," The Philosophical Review, *Vol. LXIII, No. 2 (1954). Reprinted by permission of the author and the editor of* The Philosophical Review.

[1] Strictly, here and elsewhere, "a statement made by the use of a sentence containing . . ."

sorts of cases in which it may be correct to say that a statement of one of the kinds in question is false, even though the existence-condition is not satisfied.

(A1) Suppose I make a remark of the form "The S is P," knowing that there is no S, with the deliberate intention of deceiving my hearer.[2] Suppose, for example, that I am trying to sell something and say to a prospective purchaser, "The lodger next door has offered me twice that sum," when there is no lodger next door and I know this. It would seem perfectly correct for the prospective purchaser to reply, "That's false," and to give as his reason the fact that there was no lodger next door. And it would indeed be a lame defense for me to say, "Well, it's not actually false, because, you see, since there's no such person, the question of truth or falsity doesn't arise." Both the speaker, in his attempt to deceive, and the hearer, in rejecting the speaker's assertion for the reason he gives, are relying on the fact that the speaker, by using the form of words he does, commits himself [3] to the existence of a lodger next door. The speaker exploits this logical feature of that form of words to induce a belief which he (and, as it happens, his hearer too) knows to be false. The word "false" has to a pre-eminent degree the ring of an accusation of intended deception. The hearer applies it to the speaker's assertion. What the speaker says is false, is a lie.

Clearly, then, this case calls for some modification of my thesis.

(A2) Let us now consider another kind of case of a statement containing a definite description, where nothing answers to the description. This kind of case could be characterized by saying that the statement in question would be said to be about (in one use of "about") something or someone other than the nonexistent item to which the descriptive phrase in question refers or purports to refer.[4] Suppose I am ignorantly boasting about my friend's visit to Rome and mention the king of France as one among the distinguished people he had seen there. I might say, "He had lunch with the prime minister, had an audience of the pope, and then went for a drive with the king of France." Someone might say, "Well, at least it's false (not true) that he went for a drive with the king of France—for there's no such person." Now it is important to note that in this case, where I would be said to be talking about my friend rather than about the king of France, it would also be permissible simply to *negate* the subject-predicate proposition in the ordinary way, on the strength of the nonexistence of the king of France; whereas it would not be permissible to do so in the classical case in which one is

---

[2] I am indebted to Mr. Stuart Hampshire for pointing this case out to me.
[3] Cf. above, p. 86.
[4] Messrs. H. P. Grice and G. J. Warnock have both drawn my attention to this case.

taken to be talking *about* the king of France. That is, one could say, "Well, at least he didn't go for a drive with the king of France—for there's no such person"; but one could not normally say, "The king of France isn't wise—for there's no such person." I shall refer later to this remark.

Now, to offset these concessions, I want first to make three points:

(B1) In a large number of imaginable cases in which there is nothing answering to the descriptive phrase, one would be very reluctant indeed to say either that the statement in question was true or that it was false. I have given examples elsewhere, and . . . so shall not recapitulate them here.

(B2) Even in the case of deliberate deceit, as in (A1) above, where it might be *natural* to call the statement false, it might also be highly *misleading,* unless the full circumstances, and, in particular, one's reason for calling it false, were made known. And it would be misleading because we are strongly inclined to treat the singular form "It is false that S is P" as logically equivalent to the singular form "S is not P"; and "S is not P" resembles "S is P" in that he who utters a statement of this form commits himself to the existence of S. From "It is false (untrue) that the lodger next door has offered him twice that sum" or "The statement that the lodger next door has offered him twice that sum is untrue (false)," one would be justified in concluding, "The lodger next door has not offered him twice that sum," *unless* the special circumstances, the special way, in which "false" is being used here, were made plain.

(B3) Finally, in some of the cases of the sort we are concerned with, it seems to me that, if forced to choose between calling what was said true or false, we shall be more inclined to say that it was true. Thus if, in Oxford, I declared, "The Waynflete Professor of Logic is older than I am," it would be natural to describe the situation by saying that I had confused the titles of two Oxford professors,[5] but, whichever one I had meant, what I had said about him was true. Here it may be remarked that it is the phrase "what I said" rather than the word "true" which acquires a slightly specialized use. If it is insisted that *what I actually said* rather than *what I meant* should be characterized, then resistance to applying either "true" or "false" once more becomes very strong. Similarly, perhaps, if I say, "The United States Chamber of Deputies contains representatives of two major parties," I shall be allowed to have said something true even though I have used the wrong title, a title, in fact, which applies to nothing. If "two" is replaced by "three," what I said may be called false; and the appropriateness of "false" here rests on

---

[5] The Waynflete Professor of Metaphysics and the Wykeham Professor of Logic.

the fact that what I was talking about (though misnaming or misdescribing) does not have the property I ascribed to it.

The points made so far in this section and the arguments of previous sections, may, I think, be drawn together into the following conclusions.

(i) There exists, in our ordinary use of language, a strong tendency (though not a rigid rule) for the words "true" and "false" to be used in certain ways in application to large classes of singular, universal, and particular statements, and for certain logical relationships, associated by way of mutual dependence with these ways of applying "true" and "false," to be acknowledged in our ordinary transitions and arguments. Some of the crucial relationships and applications concerned are the following:

(a) The singular form "It is false that the so-and-so is such-and-such (the S is P)" tends to be treated as logically equivalent to "The so-and-so is not such-and-such (the S is not P)."

(b) The singular form "The S is P" tends to be treated as the contradictory of "The S is not P." The universal form "All S are P," tends to be treated as the contradictory of the particular form, "Some S are not P."

(c) The two traditional universal forms tend to be treated as contraries, the two traditional particular forms as subcontraries.

(d) There is a tendency to withhold the words "true" and "false" from statements of all three kinds when, in the one case, the singular description fails to apply to anything or, in the others, the subject-class lacks members.

The point of the utmost importance here is that all these tendencies go together, are part of one and the same logical-linguistic phenomenon. They are not . . . to be separately and *differently* explained and justified. . . .

(iii) My . . . error, in the first expositions of my thesis, was to *canonize* the tendencies noted in (i) and make them into fixed and rigid rules, whereas we see they have exceptions. I think the truer account of the matter would run as follows: Those uses of "true" and "false" and of the associated logical relation words which were canonized in my unqualified doctrine of presupposition are reasonably to be regarded as the *primary* uses of these words in application to statements of the kinds in question. . . . They yield the standard and customary logic of these statements. Discussion of the truth or falsity of these statements, and comment on their logical relations, are customarily carried on against a certain background of unquestioned assumption and commitment. When these background assumptions and commitments *are* called into question, that discussion is, in general, stultified: questions of truth or falsity no longer arise, etc.[6] But *sometimes,* as in the case (A1) of deliberate deception, where the background assumption is forcibly thrust forward in a way which points accusingly at the speaker, the word "false" may acquire a *secondary* use, which collides with the primary one; and the customary logical relations, too, are involved in this collision. (I do not say that the case of deliberate deception is the only one in which this happens.) I am not sure that the other apparent exceptions mentioned above are genuine exceptions at all. What we do in cases, (B3) for example, where the speaker's *intended* reference is pretty clear, is simply to amend his statement in accordance with his guessed intentions and assess the *amended* statement for truth or falsity; we are not awarding a truth-value at all to the original statement. Case (A2) is an interesting one and merits fuller discussion than I shall give it. Clearly, however, the existence of a king of France is not, in this example, a presupposition of the whole discussion, as is the existence of the friend whose exploits I am recounting. The informal indication of this is that in no sense could the king of France be said to be the *theme* of my remarks. The formal indication is that the phrase purporting to refer to him does not figure as a grammatical subject and can be regarded as simply a *part* of a grammatical *predicate* which lacks application. But we should not find this formal indication in every such case. . . .

(v) Finally, in order to avoid misunderstanding, I must recall a point about my use of such expressions as "contradictories," "logically equivalent," "subcontraries," etc.[7] It might be thought, for example, that in saying that "All S are P" and "Some S are not P" are contradictories, I am saying that it must be the case that, of two statements of these forms with the same fillings and the same intended reference, one is true and the other false, and thus that I am saying something inconsistent with the claim that both statements may lack a truth-value. Similarly in saying that "It is false that the S is P" and "The S is not P" are logically equivalent forms, I might be thought to be saying that two statements of these forms with the same filling and the same intended reference must both be true or both be false and thus again to be contradicting my own thesis. But a very simple amendment removes all such worries. All that is required is the insertion into such definitions of these terms of the proviso that both statements have a truth-value; thus, e.g., to say that two statements are logically equivalent is to say that *if* both have a truth-value, then both must have the same truth-value.

---

[6] Cf. *Introduction to Logical Theory* (London: Methuen & Co., Ltd.; New York: John Wiley & Sons, Inc., 1952), p. 18.

[7] Cf. *Introduction to Logical Theory*, pp. 176f.

TRUTH

MICHAEL DUMMETT

Frege held that truth and falsity are the references of sentences. Sentences cannot stand for propositions (what Frege calls 'thoughts'), since the reference of a complex expression depends only on the reference of its parts; whereas if we substitute for a singular term occurring in a sentence another singular term with the same reference but a different sense, the sense of the whole sentence, i.e., the thought which it expresses, changes. The only thing which it appears *must* in these circumstances remain unchanged is the truth-value of the sentence. The expressions "is true" and "is false" look like predicates applying to propositions, and one might suppose that truth and falsity were properties of propositions; but it now appears that the relation between a proposition and its truth-value is not like that between a table and its shape, but rather like that between the sense of a definite description and the actual object for which it stands.

"Truth," Proceedings of the Aristotelian Society, 1958-1959, *Vol. LIX. Reprinted by permission of the author and the editor of the Aristotelian Society.*

To the objection that there are non-truth-functional occurrences of sentences as parts of complex sentences, e.g., clauses in indirect speech, Frege replies that in such contexts we must take ordinary singular terms as standing, not for their customary reference, but for their sense, and hence we may say that in such a context, and only then, a sentence stands for the proposition it usually expresses.

If someone asks, "But what kind of entities are these truth-values supposed to be?" we may reply that there is no more difficulty in seeing what the truth-value of a sentence may be than there is in seeing what the direction of a line may be; we have been told when two sentences have the same truth-value—when they are materially equivalent—just as we know when two lines have the same direction—when they are parallel. Nor need we waste time on the objection raised by Max Black that on Frege's theory certain sentences become meaningful which we should not normally regard as such, e.g., "If oysters are inedible, then the False." If sentences stand for truth-values, but there are also expressions standing for truth-values which are not sentences, then the objection to allowing expressions of the latter kind to stand wherever sentences can stand and vice versa is grammatical, not logical. We often use the word "thing" to provide a noun where grammar demands one and we have only an adjective, e.g., in "That was a disgraceful thing to do"; and we could introduce a verb, say "trues," to fulfil the purely grammatical function of converting a noun standing for a truth-value into a sentence standing for the same truth-value. It may be said that Frege has proved that a sentence does not ordinarily stand for a proposition, and has given a plausible argument that *if* sentences have references, they stand for truth-values, but that he has done nothing to show that sentences do have references at all. This is incorrect; Frege's demonstration that the notions of a concept (property) and a relation can be explained as special cases of the notion of a function provides a plausible argument for saying that sentences have a reference.

What *is* questionable is Frege's use of the words "truth" and "falsity" as names of the references of sentences; for by using these words rather than invented words of his own he gives the impression that by taking sentences to have a reference, with material equivalence as the criterion of identity, he has given an account of the notions of truth and falsity which we are accustomed to employ. Let us compare truth and falsity with the winning and losing of a board game. For a particular game we may imagine first formulating the rules by specifying the initial position and the permissible moves; the game comes to an end when there is no permissible move. We may then distinguish between two (or three) kinds of final positions, which we call "Win" (meaning that the player to make the first move wins), "Lose" (similarly), and, possibly, "Draw."

Unless we tacitly appeal to the usual meanings of the words "win," "lose" and "draw," this description leaves out one vital point—that it is the object of a player to win. It is part of the concept of winning a game that a player plays to win, and this part of the concept is not conveyed by a classification of the end positions into winning ones and losing ones. We can imagine a variant of chess in which it is the object of each player to be checkmated, and this would be an entirely different game; but the formal description we imagined would coincide with the formal description of chess. The whole theory of chess could be formulated with reference only to the formal description; but which theorems of this theory interested us would depend upon whether we wished to play chess or the variant game. Likewise, it is part of the concept of truth that we aim at making true statements; and Frege's theory of truth and falsity as the references of sentences leaves this feature of the concept of truth quite out of account. Frege indeed tried to bring it in afterwards, in his theory of assertion—but too late; for the sense of the sentence is not given in advance of our going in for the activity of asserting, since otherwise there could be people who expressed the same thoughts but went in instead for denying them.

A similar criticism applies to many accounts of truth and falsity or of the meanings of certain sentences in terms of truth and falsity. We cannot in general suppose that we give a proper account of a concept by describing those circumstances in which we do, and those in which we do not, make use of the relevant word, by describing the *usage* of that word; we must also give an account of the *point* of the concept, explain what we use the word *for*. Classifications do not exist in the void, but are connected always with some interest which we have, so that to assign something to one class or another will have consequences connected with this interest. A clear example is the problem of justifying a form of argument, deductive or inductive. Classification of arguments into (deductively or inductively) valid and invalid ones is not a game played merely for its own sake, although it *could* be taught without reference to any purpose or interest, say as a school exercise. Hence there is really a problem of showing that the criteria we employ for recognizing valid arguments do in fact serve the purpose we intend them to serve: the problem is not to be dismissed—as it has long been fashionable to do—by saying that we use the criteria we use.

We cannot assume that a classification effected by means of a predicate in use in a language will always have just *one* point. It may be that the classification of statements into true ones, false ones, and, perhaps, those that are neither true nor false, has one principal point, but that other subsidiary ends are served by it which make the use of the words "true" and "false" more complex than it would otherwise be. At

one time it was usual to say that we do not call ethical statements 'true'
or 'false,' and from this many consequences for ethics were held to flow.
But the question is not whether these words are in practice applied to
ethical statements, but whether, if they were so applied, the point of doing so would be the same as the point of applying them to statements of
other kinds, and, if not, in what ways it would be different. Again, to be
told that we say of a statement containing a singular term which lacks
reference that it is neither true nor false is so far only to be informed of
a point of usage; no philosophical consequences can yet be drawn. Rather,
we need to ask whether describing such a statement as neither true nor
false accords better with the general point of classifying statements as
true or false than to describe it as false. Suppose that we learn that in a
particular language such statements are described as 'false': how are we
to tell whether this shows that they use such statements differently from
ourselves or merely that "false" is not an exact translation of their word?
To say that we use singular statements in such a way that they are
neither true nor false when the subject has no reference is meant to
characterize our use of singular statements; hence it ought to be possible
to describe when in a language not containing words for "true" and
"false" singular statements would be used in the same way as we use
them, and when they would be used so as to be false when the subject
had no reference. Until we have an account of the general point of the
classification into true and false we do not know what interest attaches
to saying of certain statements that they are neither true nor false; and
until we have an account of how the truth-conditions of a statement determine its meaning the description of the meaning by stating the truth-
conditions is valueless.

A popular account of the meaning of the word "true," also deriving
from Frege, is that ⌜It is true that P⌝ has the same sense as the sentence
P. If we then ask why it is any use to have the word "true" in the
language, the answer is that we often refer to propositions indirectly, i.e.,
without expressing them, as when we say "Goldbach's conjecture" or
"what the witness said." We also generalize about propositions without
referring to any particular one, e.g., in "Everything he says is true." This
explanation cannot rank as a definition in the strict sense, since it per-
mits elimination of "is true" only when it occurs attached to a "that"-
clause, and not when attached to any other expression standing for a
proposition or to a variable; but, since every proposition can be expressed
by a sentence, this does not refute its claim to be considered as determining uniquely the sense of "is true." It might be compared with the recursive definition of "+," which enables us to eliminate the sign "+"
only when it occurs in front of a numeral, and not when it occurs in
front of any other expression for a number or in front of a variable; yet

there is a clear mathematical sense in which it specifies uniquely what operation "+" is to signify. Similarly, our explanation of "is true" determines uniquely the sense, or at least the application, of this predicate: for any given proposition there is a sentence expressing that proposition, and that sentence states the conditions under which the proposition is true.

If, as Frege thought, there exist sentences which express propositions but are neither true nor false, then this explanation appears incorrect. Suppose that P contains a singular term which has a sense but no reference: then, according to Frege, P expresses a proposition which has no truth-value. This proposition is therefore not true, and hence the statement ⌜It is true that P⌝ will be *false*. P will therefore not have the same sense as ⌜It is true that P,⌝ since the latter is false while the former is not. It is not possible to plead that ⌜It is true that P⌝ is itself neither true nor false when the singular term occurring in P lacks a reference, since the *oratio obliqua* clause ⌜that P⌝ stands for the proposition expressed by P, and it is admitted that P does have a sense and express a proposition; the singular term occurring in P has in ⌜It is true that P⌝ its indirect reference, namely its sense, and we assumed that it did have a sense. In general, it will always be inconsistent to maintain the truth of every instance of "It is true that p if and only if p" while allowing that there is a type of sentence which under certain conditions is neither true nor false. It would be possible to evade this objection by claiming that the "that"-clause in a sentence beginning "It is true that" is not an instance of *oratio obliqua;* that the word "that" here serves the purely grammatical function of transforming a sentence into a noun-clause without altering either its sense or its reference. We should then have to take phrases like "Goldbach's conjecture" and "what the witness said" as standing not for propositions but for truth-values. The expression "is true" would then be exactly like the verb "trues" which we imagined earlier; it would simply convert a noun-phrase standing for a truth-value into a sentence without altering its sense or its reference. It might be objected that this variant of Frege's account tallies badly with his saying that it is the *thought* (proposition) which is what is true or false; but we can express this point of Frege's by saying that it is the *thought,* rather than the *sentence,* which primarily stands for a truth-value. A stronger objection to the variant account is that it leans heavily on the theory of truth-values as references of sentences, while the original version depends only on the more plausible view that clauses in indirect speech stand for propositions. In any case, if there are meaningful sentences which say nothing which is true or false, then there must be *a* use of the word "true" which applies to propositions; for if we say ⌜It is neither true nor false that P,⌝ the clause ⌜that P⌝ must here be in *oratio obliqua,* otherwise the whole sentence would lack a truth-value.

Even if we do not wish to say of certain statements that they are neither true nor false, this account cannot give the *whole* meaning of the word "true." If we are to give an explanation of the word "false" parallel to our explanation of "true" we shall have to say that ⌜It is false that P⌝ has the same sense as the negation of P. In logical symbolism there exists a sign which, put in front of a sentence, forms the negation of that sentence; but in natural languages we do not have such a sign. We have to think to realize that the negation of "No-one is here" is not "No-one is not here" but "Someone is here"; there is no one rule for forming the negation of a given sentence. Now according to what principle do we recognize one sentence as the negation of another? It is natural to answer: The negation of a sentence P is that sentence which is true if and only if P is false and false if and only if P is true. But this explanation is ruled out if we want to use the notion of the negation of a sentence in order to explain the sense of the word "false." It would not solve the difficulty if we did have a general sign of negation analogous to the logical symbol, for the question would then be: How in general do we determine the sense of the negation, given the sense of the original sentence?

We encounter the same difficulty over the connective "or." We can give an account of the meaning of "and" by saying that we are in a position to assert ⌜P and Q⌝ when and only when we are in a position to assert P and in a position to assert Q. (This is not circular: one could train a dog to bark only when a bell rang *and* a light shone without presupposing that it possessed the concept of conjunction.) But, if we accept a two-valued logic, we cannot give a similar explanation of the meaning of "or." We often assert ⌜P or Q⌝ when we are not either in a position to assert P or in a position to assert Q. I use the word "we" here, meaning mankind, advisedly. If the history master gives the schoolboy a hint, saying, "It was either James I or Charles I who was beheaded," then the schoolboy is in a position to assert, "Either James I or Charles I was beheaded" without (perhaps) being in a position to assert either limb of the disjunction; but it is not this sort of case which causes the difficulty. The *ultimate* source of the schoolboy's knowledge derives from something which justifies the assertion that Charles I was beheaded; and this is all that would be required for the proposed explanation of the word "or" to be adequate. Likewise, the explanation is not impugned by cases like that in which I remember that I was talking either to Jean or to Alice, but cannot remember which. My knowledge that I was talking either to Jean or to Alice derives ultimately from the knowledge that I had at the time that I was talking to (say) Jean; the fact that the incomplete knowledge is all that survives is beside the point. Rather, the difficulty arises because we often make statements of the form ⌜P or Q⌝ when the ultimate evidence for making them, in the sense indicated, is neither evidence for the truth of P nor evidence for the truth of Q. The most striking instance of this is the fact that we are prepared to assert *any* statement of the form ⌜P or not P,⌝ even though we may have no evidence either for the truth of P or for the truth of ⌜Not P.⌝

In order to justify asserting ⌜P or not P,⌝ we appeal to the truth-table explanation of the meaning of "or." But if the whole explanation of the meanings of "true" and "false" is given by "It is true that p if and only if p" and "It is false that p if and only if not p," this appeal fails. The truth-table tells us, e.g., that from P we may infer ⌜P or Q⌝ (in particular, ⌜P or not P⌝); but *that* much we already knew from the explanation of "or" which we have rejected as insufficient. The truth-table does not show us that we are entitled to assert ⌜P or not P⌝ in every possible case, since this is to assume that every statement is either true or false; but, if our explanation of "true" and "false" is all the explanation that can be given, to say that every statement is either true or false is just to say that we are always justified in saying ⌜P or not P.⌝

We naturally think of truth-tables as giving the explanation of the sense which we attach to the sign of negation and to the connectives, an explanation which will show that we are justified in regarding certain forms of statement as logically true. It now appears that if we accept the redundancy theory of "true" and "false"—the theory that our explanation gives the whole meaning of these words—the truth-table explanation is quite unsatisfactory. More generally, we must abandon the idea which we naturally have that the notions of truth and falsity play an essential role in any account either of the meaning of statements in general or of the meaning of a particular statement. The conception pervades the thought of Frege that the general form of explanation of the sense of a statement consists in laying down the conditions under which it is true and those under which it is false (or better: saying that it is false under all other conditions); this same conception is expressed in the *Tractatus* in the words, "In order to be able to say that 'p' is true (or false), I must have determined under what conditions I call 'p' true, and this is how I determine the sense of the sentence" (4.063). But in order that someone should gain from the explanation that P is true in such-and-such circumstances an understanding of the sense of P, he must already know what it means to say of P that it is true. If when he inquires into this he is told that the only explanation is that to say that P is true is the same as to assert P, it will follow that in order to understand what is meant by saying that P is true, he must already know the sense of asserting P, which was precisely what was supposed to be being explained to him.

We thus have either to supplement the redundancy theory or to give up many of our preconceptions about truth and falsity. It has become a commonplace to say that there cannot be a criterion of truth. The argument is that we determine the sense of a sentence by laying down the conditions under which it is true, so that we could not first know the sense of a sentence and then apply some criterion to decide in what circumstances it was true. In the same sense there could not be a criterion for what constitutes the winning of a game, since learning what constitutes winning it is an essential part of learning what the game is. This does not mean that there may not be in any sense a theory of truth. For a particular bounded language, if it is free of ambiguity and inconsistency, it must be possible to characterize the true sentences of the language; somewhat as, for a given game, we can say which moves are winning moves. (A language is bounded if we may not introduce into it new words or new senses for old words.) Such a characterization would be recursive, defining truth first for the simplest possible sentences, and then for sentences built out of others by the logical operations employed in the language; this is what is done for formalized languages by a truth-definition. The redundancy theory gives the general form of such a truth-definition, though in particular cases more informative definitions might be given.

Now we have seen that to say for each particular game what winning it consists in is not to give a satisfactory account of the concept of winning a game. What makes us use the same term "winning" for each of these various activities is that the point of every game is that each player tries to do what for that game constitutes winning; i.e., what constitutes winning always plays the same part in determining what playing the game consists in. Similarly, what the truth of a statement consists in always plays the same role in determining the sense of that statement, and a theory of truth must be possible in the sense of an account of what that role is. I shall not now attempt such an account; I claim, however, that such an account would justify the following. A statement, so long as it is not ambiguous or vague, divides all possible states of affairs into just *two* classes. For a given state of affairs, either the statement is used in such a way that a man who asserted it but envisaged that state of affairs as a possibility would be held to have spoken misleadingly, or the assertion of the statement would not be taken as expressing the speaker's exclusion of that possibility. If a state of affairs of the first kind obtains, the statement is false; if all actual states of affairs are of the second kind, it is true. It is thus *prima facie* senseless to say of any statement that in such-and-such a state of affairs it would be neither true nor false.

The sense of a statement is determined by knowing in what circumstances it is true and in what false. Likewise the sense of a command is determined by knowing what constitutes obedience to it and what disobedience; and the sense of a bet by knowing when the bet is won and when it is lost. Now there may be a gap between the winning of a bet and the losing of it, as with a conditional bet; can there be a similar gap between obedience and disobedience to a command, or between the truth and falsity of a statement? There is a distinction between a conditional bet and a bet on the truth of a material conditional; if the antecedent is unfulfilled, in the first case the bet is off—it is just as if no bet had been made—but in the second case the bet is won. A conditional command where the antecedent is in the power of the person given the order (e.g., a mother says to a child, "If you go out, wear your coat") is always like a bet on the material conditional; it is equivalent to the command to ensure the truth of the material conditional, viz., "Do not go out without your coat." We cannot say that if the child does not go out, it is just as if no command had been given, since it may be that, unable to find his coat, he stayed in in order to comply with the command.

Can a distinction parallel to that for bets be drawn for conditional commands where the antecedent is not in the person's power? I contend that the distinction which looks as if it could be drawn is in fact void of significance. There are two distinct kinds of consequence of making a bet, winning it and losing; to determine what is to involve one of these is not yet to determine completely what is to involve the other. But there is only one kind of consequence of giving a command, namely that, provided one had the right to give it in the first place, one acquires a right to punish or at least reprobate disobedience. It might be thought that punishment and reward were distinct consequences of a command in the same sense that paying money and receiving it are distinct consequences of a bet; but this does not tally with the role of commands in our society. The right to a reward is not taken to be an automatic consequence of obedience to a command, as the *right* to reproach is an automatic consequence of disobedience; if a reward is given, this is an act of grace, just as it is an act of grace if the punishment or reproach is withheld. Moreover, any action deliberately taken in order to comply with the command (to avoid disobedience to it) has the same claim to be rewarded as any other; hence to determine what constitutes disobedience to the command is thereby to determine what sort of behavior might be rewarded, without the need for any further decision. If the child stays in because he cannot find his coat, this behavior is as meritorious as if he goes out remembering to wear it; and if he forgets all about the order, but wears his coat for some other reason, this behavior no more deserves commendation than if he chooses, for selfish reasons, to remain indoors. Where the antecedent is not in the person's power, it is indeed possible to regard the conditional command as analogous to the conditional bet;

but since obedience to a command has no consequence of its own other than that of avoiding the punishment due for disobedience, there is not for such commands any significant distinction parallel to that between conditional bets and bets about a material conditional. If we regarded obedience to a command as giving a right to a reward, we could then introduce such a distinction for commands whose antecedent was in the person's power. Thus the mother might use the form, "If you go out, wear your coat," as involving that if the child went out with his coat he would be rewarded, if he went out without it he would be punished, and if he stayed indoors—even in order to comply with the command—he would be neither punished nor rewarded; while the form, "Do not go out without your coat," would involve his being rewarded if he stayed indoors.

Statements are like commands (as we use them) and not like bets; the making of a statement has, as it were, only one kind of consequence. To see this, let us imagine a language which contains conditional statements but has no counterfactual form (counterfactuals would introduce irrelevant complications). Two alternative accounts are suggested of the way in which conditionals are used in this language: one, that they are used to make statements conditionally; the other, that they represent the material conditional. On the first interpretation, a conditional statement is like a conditional bet: if the antecedent is fulfilled, then the statement is treated as if it had been an unconditional assertion of the consequent, and is said to be true or false accordingly; if the antecedent is not fulfilled, then it is just as if no statement, true or false, had been made at all. On the second interpretation, if the antecedent is not fulfilled, then the statement is said to be true. How are we to settle which of these two accounts is the correct one? If statements are really like bets and not like commands; if there are two distinct kinds of consequence which may follow the making of a statement, those that go with calling the statement 'true' and those that go with calling it 'false,' so that there may be a gap between these two kinds of consequence; then we ought to be able to find something which decides between the two accounts as definite as the financial transaction which distinguishes a bet on the truth of the material conditional from a conditional bet. It is no use asking whether these people *say* that the man who has made a conditional statement whose antecedent turns out false said something true or that he said nothing true or false: they may have no words corresponding to "true" and "false"; and if they do, how could we be sure that the correspondence was exact? If their using the words "true" and "false" is to have the slightest significance, there must be some difference in their behavior which goes with their saying "true" or "neither true nor false" in this case.

It is evident on reflection that there is nothing in what they do which could distinguish between the two alternative accounts; the distinction between them is as empty as the analogous distinction for conditional commands whose antecedent is not in the person's power. In order to fix the sense of an utterance, we do not need to make two separate decisions —when to say that a true statement has been made and when to say that a false statement has been made; rather, any situation in which nothing obtains which is taken as a case of its being false may be regarded as a case of its being true, just as someone who behaves so as not to disobey a command may be regarded as having obeyed it. The point becomes clearer when we look at it in the following way. If it makes sense in general to suppose that a certain form of statement is so used that in certain circumstances it is true, in others false, and in yet others nothing has been said true or false, then we can imagine that a form of conditional was used in this way (von Wright actually holds that *we* use conditionals in this way). If P turns out true, then ⌜If P, then Q⌝ is said to be true or false according as Q is true or false, while if P turns out false we say that nothing was said true or false. Let us contrast this with what Frege and Strawson say about the use in our langauge of statements containing a singular term. If there is an object for which the singular term stands, then the statement is true or false according as the predicate does or does not apply to that object, but if there is no such object, then we have not said anything true or false. Now do these accounts tell us the sense of sentences of these two kinds?—that is, do they tell us how these statements are used, what is *done* by making statements of these forms? Not at all, for an essential feature of their use has not yet been laid down. Someone uttering a conditional statement of the kind described may very well have no opinion as to whether the antecedent was going to turn out true or false; that is, he is not taken as having misused the statement or misled his hearers if he envisages it as a possibility that that case will arise in which he is said not to have made a statement true or false. All that he conveys by uttering the conditional statement is that he excludes the possibility that the case will arise in which he is said to have said something false, namely that antecedent is true and consequent false. With the case of a singular statement it is quite different. Here someone is definitely either misusing the form of statement or misleading his hearers if he envisages it as a possibility that that case will arise in which what he said will be said to be neither true nor false, namely that the singular term has no reference. He conveys more by making the statement than just that he excludes the possibility of its being false; he commits himself to its being true.

Are we then to say that laying down the truth-conditions for a sentence is not sufficient to determine its sense, that something further will have to be stipulated as well? Rather than say this we should abandon the notions of truth and falsity altogether. In order to characterize the sense of expressions of our two forms, only a twofold classification of possible relevant circumstances is necessary. We need to distinguish those states of affairs such that if the speaker envisaged them as possibilities he would be held to be either misusing the statement or misleading his hearers, and those of which this is not the case: and *one* way of using the words "true" and "false" would be to call states of affairs of the former kind those in which the statement was false and the others those in which the statement was true. For our conditional statements, the distinction would be between those states of affairs in which the statement was said to be false and those in which we said that it would either be true or else neither true nor false. For singular statements, the distinction would be between those states of affairs in which we said that the statement would either be false or else neither true nor false, and those in which it was true. To grasp the sense or use of these forms of statement, the twofold classification is quite sufficient; the threefold classification with which we started is entirely beside the point. Thus, on *one* way of using the words "true" and "false," we should, instead of distinguishing between the conditional statement's being true and its being neither true nor false, have distinguished between two different ways in which it could be true; and instead of distinguishing between the singular statement's being false and its being neither true nor false, we should have distinguished between two different ways in which it could be false.

This gives us a hint at a way of explaining the role played by truth and falsity in determining the sense of a statement. We have not yet seen what point there may be in distinguishing between different ways in which a statement may be true or between different ways in which it may be false, or, as we might say, between degrees of truth and falsity. The point of such distinctions does not lie in anything to do with the sense of the statement itself, but has to do with the way in which it enters into complex statements. Let us imagine that in the language of which the conditional statements we considered form a part there exists a sign of negation, i.e., a word which, placed in front of a statement, forms another statement; I call it a sign of negation because in most cases it forms a statement which we should regard as being used as the contradictory of the original statement. Let us suppose, however, that when placed in front of a conditional statement ⌜If P, then Q,⌝ it forms a statement which is used in the same way as the statement ⌜If P, then not Q.⌝ Then if we describe the use of the conditionals by reference to a twofold classification only, i.e., in the same way as we describe a material conditional, we shall be unable to give a truth-functional account of the behavior of their sign "not." That is, we should have the tables:

P	Q	⌜If P, then Q⌝	⌜Not: if P, then Q⌝
T	T	T	F
T	F	F	T
F	T	T	T
F	F	T	T

in which the truth-value of ⌜Not: if P, then Q⌝ is not determined by the truth-value of ⌜If P, then Q.⌝ If, on the other hand, we revert to our original threefold classification, marking the case in which we said that no statement true or false had been made by "X," then we have the tables:

P	Q	⌜If P, then Q⌝	⌜Not: if P, then Q⌝
T	T	T	F
T	F	F	T
F	T	X	X
F	F	X	X

which can be quite satisfactorily accounted for by giving the table for "not":

R	⌜Not R⌝
T	F
X	X
F	T

(I have assumed that the statements P and Q take only the values T and F.) It now becomes quite natural to think of "T" as representing "true," "F" "false" and "X" "neither true nor false." Then we can say that their symbol "not" really is a sign of negation, since ⌜Not P⌝ is true when and only when P is false and false when and only when P is true. We must not forget, however, that the justification for distinguishing between the cases in which a conditional was said to have the value T and the cases in which it was said to have the value X was simply the possibility, created by this distinction, of treating "not" truth-functionally. In the same way if we have in a language an expression which normally functions as a sign of negation, but the effect of prefacing a singular statement with this expression is to produce a statement whose utterance still commits the speaker to there being an object for which the singular term stands, it is very natural to distinguish between two kinds of falsity a singular statement may have: that when the singular term has a reference, but the predicate does not apply to it, and that when the singular term lacks a reference. Let us represent the case in which the singular term has no reference by the symbol "Y," and let us suppose S to be a singular statement. Then we have the table:

S	⌐Not S⌐
T	F
Y	Y
F	T

Here again it is natural to think of "T" as representing "true," "F" "false" and "Y" "neither true nor false."

There is no necessity to use the words "true" and "false" as suggested above, so that we have to interpret X as a kind of truth and Y as a kind of falsity. Logicians who study many-valued logics have a term which can be employed here: they would say that T and X are 'designated' truth-values and F and Y 'undesignated' ones. (In a many-valued logic those formulas are considered valid which have a designated value for every assignment of values to their sentence-letters.) The points to observe are just these: (i) The sense of a sentence is determined wholly by knowing the case in which it has a designated value and the cases in which it has an undesignated one. (ii) Finer distinctions between different designated values or different undesignated ones, however naturally they come to us, are justified only if they are needed in order to give a truth-functional account of the formation of complex statements by means of operators. (iii) In *most* philosophical discussions of truth and falsity, what we really have in mind is the distinction between a designated and an undesignated value, and hence choosing the names "truth" and "falsity" for particular designated and undesignated values respectively will only obscure the issue. (iv) Saying that in certain circumstances a statement is neither true nor false does not determine whether the statement is in that case to count as having an undesignated or a designated value, i.e., whether someone who asserts the statement is or is not taken as excluding the possibility that that case obtains.

Baffled by the attempt to describe in general the relation between language and reality, we have nowadays abandoned the correspondence theory of truth, and justify our doing so on the score that it was an attempt to state a *criterion* of truth in the sense in which this cannot be done. Nevertheless, the correspondence theory expresses one important feature of the concept of truth which is not expressed by the law "It is true that p if and only if p" and which we have so far left quite out of account: that a statement is true only if there is something in the world *in virtue of which* it is true. Although we no longer accept the correspondence theory, we remain realists *au fond;* we retain in our thinking a fundamentally realist conception of truth. Realism consists in the belief that for any statement there must be something in virtue of which either it or its negation is true: it is only on the basis of this belief that we can justify the idea that truth and falsity play an essential role in the notion of the meaning of a statement, that the general form of an explanation of meaning is a statement of the truth-conditions.

To see the importance of this feature of the concept of truth, let us envisage a dispute over the logical validity of the statement "Either Jones was brave or he was not." A imagines Jones to be a man, now dead, who never encountered danger in his life. B retorts that it could still be true that Jones was brave, namely, if it is true that if Jones *had* encountered danger, he would have acted bravely. A agrees with this, but still maintains that it does not need to be the case that either "Jones was brave" = "If Jones had encountered danger, he would have acted bravely" nor "Jones was not brave" = "If Jones had encountered danger, he would not have acted bravely" is true. For, he argues, it might be the case that however many facts we knew of the kind which we should normally regard as grounds for asserting such counterfactual conditionals, we should still know nothing which would be a ground for asserting either. It is clear that B cannot agree that this is a possibility and yet continue to insist that all the same either "Jones was brave" or "Jones was not brave" is true; for he would then be committed to holding that a statement may be true even though there is nothing whatever such that, if we knew of it, we should count it as evidence or as a ground for the truth of the statement, and this is absurd. (It may be objected that there are assertions for which it would be out of place to ask one who made them for his evidence or grounds; but for *such* assertions the speaker must always either be in a position to make or in a position to deny them.) If B still wishes to maintain the necessity of "Either Jones was brave or he was not," he will have to hold either that there must be some fact of the sort to which we usually appeal in discussing counterfactuals which, if we knew it, would decide us in favor either of the one counterfactual or of the other; or else that there is some fact of an extraordinary kind, perhaps known only to God. In the latter case he imagines a kind of spiritual mechanism—Jones' character—which determines how he acts in each situation that arises; his acting in such-and-such a way reveals to us the state of this spiritual mechanism, which was however already in place before its observable effects were displayed in his behavior. B would then argue thus: If Jones *had* encountered danger, he would either have acted bravely or have acted like a coward. Suppose he had acted bravely. This would then have shown us that he was brave; but he would *already* have been brave before his courage was revealed by his behavior. That is, either his character included the quality of courage or it did not, and his character determines his behavior. We know his character only indirectly, through its effects on his behavior; but each character-trait must be *there* within him independently of whether it reveals itself to us or not.

Anyone of a sufficient degree of sophistication will reject B's belief in a spiritual mechanism; either he will be a materialist and substitute for it an equally blind belief in a physiological mechanism, or he will accept A's conclusion that "Either Jones was brave or he was not" is not logically necessary. His ground for rejecting B's argument is that if such a statement as "Jones was brave" is true, it must be true in virtue of the sort of fact we have been taught to regard as justifying us in asserting it. It cannot be true in virtue of a fact of some quite different sort of which we can have no direct knowledge, for otherwise the statement "Jones was brave" would not have the meaning that *we* have given it. In accepting A's position he makes a small retreat from realism; he abandons a realist view of character.

In order, then, to decide whether a realist account of truth can be given for statements of some particular kind, we have to ask whether for such a statement P it must be the case that if we knew sufficiently many facts of the kind we normally treat as justifying us in asserting P, we should be in a position either to assert P or to assert ⌜Not P⌝: if so, then it can truly be said that there must either be something in virtue of which P is true or something in virtue of which it is false. It is easy to overlook the force of the phrase "sufficiently many." Consider the statement "A city will never be built on this spot." Even if we have an oracle which can answer every question of the kind, "Will there be a city here in 1990?" "In 2100?" etc., we might never be in a position either to declare the statement true or to declare it false. Someone may say: That is only because you are assuming the knowledge of only finitely many answers of the oracle; but if you knew the oracle's answers to *all* these questions, you would be able to decide the truth-value of the statement. But what would it mean to know infinitely many facts? It could mean that the oracle gave a direct answer "No" to the question, "Will a city ever be built here?": but to assume this is just like B's assumption of the existence of a hidden spiritual mechanism. It might mean that we had an argument to show the falsity of ⌜A city will be built here in the year N⌝ irrespective of the value of N, e.g., if 'here' is the North Pole: but no one would suggest that it must be the case that either the oracle will give an affirmative answer to some question of the form "Will there be a city here in the year . . . . ?" or we can find a general argument for a negative answer. Finally, it could mean that we were *able* to answer every question of the form, "Will there be a city here in the year . . . . ?": but having infinite knowledge in *this* sense will place us in no better position than when we had the oracle.

We thus arrive at the following position. We are entitled to say that a statement P must be either true or false, that there must be something in virtue of which either it is true or it is false, only when P is a statement of such a kind that we could in a finite time bring ourselves into a position in which we were justified either in asserting or in denying P; that is, when P is an effectively decidable statement. This limitation is not trivial: there is an immense range of statements which, like "Jones was brave," are concealed conditionals, or which, like "A city will never be built here," contain—explicitly or implicitly—an unlimited generality, and which therefore fail the test.

What I have done here is to transfer to ordinary statements what the intuitionists say about mathematical statements. The sense of e.g., the existential quantifier is determined by considering what sort of fact makes an existential statement true, and this means: the sort of fact which we have been taught to regard as justifying us in asserting an existential statement. What would make the statement that there exists an odd perfect number true would be some particular number's being both odd and perfect; hence the assertion of the existential statement must be taken as a claim to be able to assert some one of the singular statements. We are thus justified in asserting that there is a number with a certain property only if we have a method for finding a particular number with that property. Likewise, the sense of a universal statement is given by the sort of consideration we regard as justifying us in asserting it: namely we can assert that every number has a certain property if we have a general method for showing, for any arbitrary number, that it has that property. Now what if someone insists that either the statement "There is an odd perfect number" is true, or else every perfect number is even? He is justified if he knows of a procedure which will lead him in a finite time either to the determination of a particular odd perfect number or to a general proof that a number assumed to be perfect is even. But if he knows of no such procedure, then he is trying to attach to the statement "Every perfect number is even" a meaning which lies *beyond* that provided by the training we are given in the use of universal statements; he wants to say, as B said of "Jones was brave," that its truth may lie in a region directly accessible only to God, which human beings can never survey.

We learn the sense of the logical operators by being trained to *use* statements containing them, i.e., to assert such statements under certain conditions. Thus we learn to assert ⌜P and Q⌝ when we can assert P and can assert Q; to assert ⌜P or Q⌝ when we can assert P or can assert Q; to assert ⌜For some n, $F(n)$⌝ when we can assert ⌜$F(0)$⌝ or can assert ⌜$F(1)$⌝ or .... We learn to assert ⌜For every n, $F(n)$⌝ when we can assert ⌜$F(0)$⌝ and ⌜$F(1)$⌝ and ....; and to say that we can assert all of these means that we have a general method for establishing ⌜F(x)⌝ irrespective of the value of *x*. Here we have abandoned altogether the attempt to explain the meaning of a statement by laying down its truth-conditions. *We no longer explain the sense of a statement by stipulating its truth-value in terms of the truth-values of its constituents, but by stipulating when it may be asserted in terms of the conditions under which its constituents may be asserted.* The justification for this change is that this is how we in fact learn to use these statements: furthermore, the notions of truth and falsity cannot be satisfactorily explained so as to form a basis for an account of meaning once we leave the realm of effectively decidable statements. One result of this shift in our account of meaning is that, unless we are dealing only with effectively decidable statements, certain formulas which appeared in the two-valued logic to be logical laws no longer rank as such, in particular the law of excluded middle: this is rejected, not on the ground that there is a middle truth-value, but because meaning, and hence validity, is no longer to be explained in terms of truth-values.

Intuitionists speak of mathematics in a highly antirealist (antiplatonist) way: for them it is *we* who construct mathematics; it is not already *there* waiting for us to discover. An extreme form of such constructivism is found in Wittgenstein's *Remarks on the Foundations of Mathematics.* This makes it appear as though the intuitionist rejection of an account of the meaning of mathematical statements in terms of truth and falsity could not be generalized for other regions of discourse, since even if there is no independent mathematical reality answering to our mathematical statements, there is an independent reality answering to statements of other kinds. On the other hand the exposition of intuitionism I have just given was not based on a rejection of the Fregean notion of a mathematical reality waiting to be discovered, but only on considerations about meaning. Now certainly someone who accepts the intuitionist standpoint in mathematics will not be inclined to adopt the platonist picture. Must he then go to the other extreme, and have the picture of our creating mathematics as we go along? To adopt this picture involves thinking with Wittgenstein that we are *free* in mathematics at every point; no step we take has been forced on us by a necessity external to us, but has been freely chosen. This picture is not the only alternative. If we think that mathematical results are in some sense imposed on us from without, we could have instead the picture of a mathematical reality not already in existence but as it were coming into being as we probe. Our investigations bring into existence what was not there before, but what they bring into existence is not of our own making.

Whether this picture is right or wrong for mathematics, it is available for other regions of reality as an alternative to the realist conception of the world. This shows how it is possible to hold that the intuitionist substitution of an account of the *use* of a statement for an account of its truth-conditions as the general form of explanation of meaning should be applied to all realms of discourse without thinking that we create the world; we can abandon realism without falling into subjective idealism. This substitution does not, of course, involve dropping the words "true" and "false," since for most ordinary contexts the account of these words embodied in the laws "It is true that p if and only if p" and "It is false that p if and only if not p" is quite sufficient: but it means facing the consequences of admitting that this is the *whole* explanation of the sense of these words, and this involves dethroning truth and falsity from their central place in philosophy and in particular in the theory of meaning. Of course the doctrine that meaning is to be explained in terms of use is the cardinal doctrine of the later Wittgenstein; but I do not think the point of this doctrine has so far been generally understood.

SELECTED BIBLIOGRAPHY

CORRESPONDENCE THEORY

Acton, H. B., "The Correspondence Theory of Truth," *Proceedings of the Aristotelian Society, 1934-1935,* Vol. XXXV.

Austin, J. L., "Unfair to Facts," *Philosophical Papers,* Chap. 5. Oxford: The Clarendon Press, 1961.

Baylis, C. A., "Facts, Propositions, Exemplification and Truth," *Mind,* Vol. LVII (1948).

Black, M., "A Propos of 'Facts,' " *Analysis,* Vol. I, No. 3 (1934).

Cousin, D. R., "Truth," *Proceedings of the Aristotelian Society,* Supp. Vol. XXIV (1950).

Furberg, Mats, *Locutionary and Illocutionary Acts: A Main Theme in J. L. Austin's Philosophy,* Chap. 3. Göteborg: Acta Universitatis Gothoburgensis, 1963.

Hamlyn, D. W., "The Correspondence Theory of Truth," *Philosophical Quarterly,* Vol. XII (1962).

Hampshire, S., "Ideas, Propositions and Signs," *Proceedings of the Aristotelian Society, 1939-1940,* Vol. XL.

Herbst, P., "The Nature of Facts," *Australasian Journal of Philosophy,* Vol. XXX (1952). Reprinted in *Essays in Conceptual Analysis,* A. Flew, ed. New York: St. Martin's Press, 1956.

Lucas, J. R., "On not Worshipping Facts," *Philosophical Quarterly,* Vol. VIII (1958).

Moore, G. E., "Facts and Propositions," *Proceedings of the Aristotelian Society,* Supp. Vol. VII (1927). Reprinted in *Philosophical Papers.* New York: The Macmillan Company, 1959.

——, *Some Main Problems of Philosophy,* Chaps. 3, 14-15, and 17. New York: The Macmillan Company, 1953.

Russell, B., *Philosophical Essays,* Chap. 7. London: Longmans, Green & Company, Ltd., 1910.

——, "The Philosophy of Logical Atomism," *Monist,* Vol. XXVIII (1918) and Vol. XXIX (1919). Reprinted in *Logic and Knowledge,* R. C. Marsh, ed. London: George Allen & Unwin, 1956.

——, *The Problems of Philosophy,* Chap. 12. London: Oxford University Press, 1912.

——, "On Propositions: What They Are and How They Mean," *Proceedings of the Aristotelian Society,* Supp. Vol. II (1919). Reprinted in *Logic and Knowledge, op. cit.*

Ryle, G., "Are There Propositions?" *Proceedings of the Aristotelian Society, 1929-1930,* Vol. XXX.

Sellars, W., "Truth and 'Correspondence,'" *Journal of Philosophy,* Vol. LIX (1962). Reprinted in *Science, Perception and Reality.* New York: The Humanities Press, 1963.

Shorter, J. M., "Facts, Logical Atomism and Reducibility," *Australasian Journal of Philosophy,* Vol. XL (1962).

Sørensen, H. S., "An Analysis of 'To Be' and 'To Be True': A Linguist's Approach to the Problem," *Analysis,* Vol. XIX, No. 6 (1959).

Wittgenstein, L., *Tractatus Logico-Philosophicus,* D. F. Pears and B. F. McGuinness, trans. New York: The Humanities Press, 1961.

Woozley, A. D., *Theory of Knowledge: An Introduction,* Chap. 6. London: Hutchinson & Co., Ltd., 1949.

COHERENCE THEORY

Ayer, A. J., "Verification and Experience," *Proceedings of the Aristotelian Society, 1936-1937,* Vol. XXXVII.

Blanshard, B., *The Nature of Thought,* Vol. II, Chaps. 25-27. New York: The Macmillan Company, 1940.

Bradley, F. H., *Appearance and Reality: A Metaphysical Essay,* 2nd ed., Chaps. 15 and 24. Oxford: The Clarendon Press, 1897.

——, *Essays on Truth and Reality.* Oxford: The Clarendon Press, 1914.

Broad, C. D., "Mr. Bradley on Truth and Reality," *Mind,* Vol. XXIII (1914).

Ewing, A. C., *Idealism: A Critical Survey,* Chap. 5. London: Methuen & Co., Ltd., 1934.

Hempel, C. G., "On the Logical Positivists' Theory of Truth," *Analysis*, Vol. II, No. 4 (1935).

———, "Some Remarks on 'Facts' and Propositions," *Ibid.*, Vol. II, No. 6 (1935).

Joachim, H. H., *The Nature of Truth*. Oxford: The Clarendon Press, 1906.

Russell, B., *An Inquiry into Meaning and Truth*, Chap. 10. London: George Allen & Unwin, 1940.

———, *Philosophical Essays, op. cit.*, Chap. 6.

———, "On Verification," *Proceedings of the Aristotelian Society, 1937-1938*, Vol. XXXVIII.

Schlick, M., "Facts and Propositions," *Analysis*, Vol. II, No. 5 (1935). Reprinted in *Philosophy and Analysis*. M. Macdonald, ed. Oxford: Basil Blackwell & Mott, Ltd., 1954.

Stout, G. F., "Bradley on Truth and Falsity," *Mind*, Vol. XXXIV (1925). Reprinted in *Studies in Philosophy and Psychology*. London: Macmillan and Co., Ltd., 1930.

Wollheim, R., *F. H. Bradley*, Chap. 4. Baltimore: Penguin Books, Inc., 1959.

Woozley, A. D., *Theory of Knowledge, op. cit.*, Chap. 7.

PRAGMATIC THEORY

Aiken, H. D., "American Pragmatism Reconsidered: Part II, William James," *Commentary*, Vol. XXXIV, No. 2 (1962).

James, W., *Pragmatism*, Lectures II and VI. New York: David McKay Co., Inc., 1907.

Moore, G. E., "William James' 'Pragmatism,'" *Proceedings of the Aristotelian Society, 1907-1908*, Vol. VIII. Reprinted in *Philosophical Studies*. London: Routledge & Kegan Paul, Ltd., 1922.

Perkins, M., "Notes on the Pragmatic Theory of Truth," *Journal of Philosophy*, Vol. XLIX (1952).

Richman, R. J., "Truth and Verifiability," *Ibid.*, Vol. L (1953).

Russell, B., *Philosophical Essays, op. cit.*, Chap. 5.

REDUNDANCY THEORY

Ayer, A. J., *Language, Truth and Logic* (2nd ed.), Chap. 5. London: Victor Gollancz, Ltd., 1946.

Ayer, A. J., "Truth," *Revue internationale de philosophie,* Vol. VII, No. 25 (1953).

——, "Truth," in *The Concept of a Person and Other Essays.* New York: St. Martin's Press, 1963.

Ezorsky, G., "Truth in Context," *Journal of Philosophy,* Vol. LX (1963).

Moore, G. E., "Facts and Propositions," *op. cit.*

Ramsey, F. P., "Facts and Propositions," *Proceedings of the Aristotelian Society,* Supp. Vol. VII (1927). Reprinted in *The Foundations of Mathematics.* London: Routledge & Kegan Paul, Ltd., 1931.

SEMANTIC CONCEPTION

Black, M., "The Semantic Definition of Truth," *Analysis,* Vol. VIII, No. 4 (1948). Reprinted in *Language and Philosophy.* Ithaca, N. Y.: Cornell University Press, 1949.

Cousin, D. R., "Carnap's Theories of Truth," *Mind,* Vol. LIX (1950).

von Juhos, B., "The Truth of Empirical Statements," *Analysis,* Vol. IV, No. 5 (1937).

Pap, A., "Note on the 'Semantic' and the 'Absolute' Concept of Truth," *Philosophical Studies,* Vol. III (1952).

——, "Propositions, Sentences and the Semantic Definition of Truth," *Theoria,* Vol. XX (1954).

Tarski, A., "The Semantic Conception of Truth," *Philosophy and Phenomenological Research,* Vol. IV (1944). Reprinted in *Readings in Philosophical Analysis,* H. Feigl and W. Sellars, eds. (New York: Appleton-Century-Crofts, Inc., 1949) and *Semantics and the Philosophy of Language,* L. Linsky, ed. (Urbana, Ill.: University of Illinois Press, 1952).

Thomson, J. F., "A Note on Truth," *Analysis,* Vol. IX, No. 5 (1949).

STRAWSON'S VIEW

Ezorsky, G., "Truth in Context," *op. cit.*

Furberg, Mats, *Locutionary and Illocutionary Acts, op. cit.,* Chap. 3.

Geach, P., *Mental Acts,* Chap. 21. New York: The Humanities Press, 1957.

Kincade, J., "On the Performatory Theory of Truth," *Mind,* Vol. LXVII (1958).

Searle, J. R., "Meaning and Speech Acts," *Philosophical Review,* Vol. LXXI (1962).

Strawson, P. F., "Truth," *Analysis,* Vol. IX, No. 6 (1949). Reprinted in *Philosophy and Analysis, op. cit.*

Walsh, W. H., "A Note on Truth," *Mind,* Vol. LXI (1952).

OTHER VIEWS

Mayo, B., "Truth as Appraisal," *Mind,* Vol. LXVIII (1959).

Savery, B., "The Emotive Theory of Truth," *Ibid.,* Vol. LXIV (1955).

White, A. R., "Truth as Appraisal," *Ibid.,* Vol. LXVI (1957).

TOPICS RAISED IN LAST THREE SELECTIONS

Danto, A. C., "A Note on Expressions of the Referring Sort," *Mind,* Vol. LXVII (1958).

Peterson, S., "All John's Children," *Philosophical Quarterly,* Vol. X (1960).

Sellars, W., "Presupposing," *Philosophical Review,* Vol. LXIII (1954).

Slater, B. A., "Talking about Something," *Analysis,* Vol. XXIII, No. 3 (1963).

Strawson, P. F., "On Referring," *Mind,* Vol. LIX (1950). Reprinted in *Essays in Conceptual Analysis, op. cit.*

———, "Singular Terms and Predication," *Journal of Philosophy,* Vol. LVIII (1961).

———, *Individuals,* Chap. 6. London: Methuen & Co., Ltd., 1959.

MISCELLANEOUS

Albritton, R., "Present Truth and Future Contingency," *Philosophical Review,* Vol. LXVI (1957).

Austin, J. L., *How to do things with Words,* pp. 139-144. Oxford: The Clarendon Press, 1962.

Baylis, C. A., "Are Some Propositions Neither True Nor False?" *Philosophy of Science,* Vol. III (1936).

Donnellan, K. S., "A Note on the Liar Paradox," *Philosophical Review,* Vol. LXVI (1957).

Goddard, L., " 'True' and 'Provable,' " *Mind,* Vol. LXVII (1958).

Harre, R., " '. . . Is True,' " *Australasian Journal of Philosophy,* Vol. XXXV (1957).

Kaufmann, W., *Critique of Religion and Philosophy,* Sec. III. New York: Harper & Row, Publishers, Inc., 1958.

King-Farlow, J., "Truth Preference and Neuter Propositions," *Philosophy of Science,* Vol. XXX (1963).

Parsons, C. and H. R. Kohl, "Self-Reference, Truth, and Provability," *Mind,* Vol. LXIX (1960).

Pears, D. F., "Time, Truth and Inference," *Proceedings of the Aristotelian Society, 1950-1951,* Vol. LI. Reprinted in *Essays in Conceptual Analysis, op. cit.*

Skinner, R. C., "The Paradox of the Liar," *Mind,* Vol. LXVIII (1959).

Taylor, R., "The Problem of Future Contingencies," *Philosophical Review,* Vol. LXVI (1957).

Toms, E., "The Liar Paradox," *Ibid.,* Vol. LXV (1956).

——, "Reply to a Note on the Liar Paradox," *Ibid.,* Vol. LXVII (1958).

Williams, D. C., "The Sea Fight Tomorrow," in *Structure, Meaning, and Method: Essays in Honor of Henry M. Sheffer,* P. Henle, H. M. Kallen, and S. K. Langer, eds. New York: The Liberal Arts Press, 1951.